COMMUNITY UNDER ATTACK

The Struggle for Survival in the Coalfield Communities of Britain

Ken Coates, MEP
and
Michael Barratt Brown

with an introduction by
Ludivina Garcia Arias, MEP
President of EURACOM

SPOKESMAN

First published in Great Britain in 1997 by
Spokesman
Bertrand Russell House
Gamble Street
Nottingham, England
Tel. 0115 9708318
Fax. 0115 9420433

British Library Cataloguing in Publication Data available on request from the
British Library.

ISBN 0-85124-612-5 cloth
ISBN 0-85124-613-3 paper

Printed by the Russell Press Ltd., Nottingham
(Tel. 0115 9784505)

Britain's Coalfields

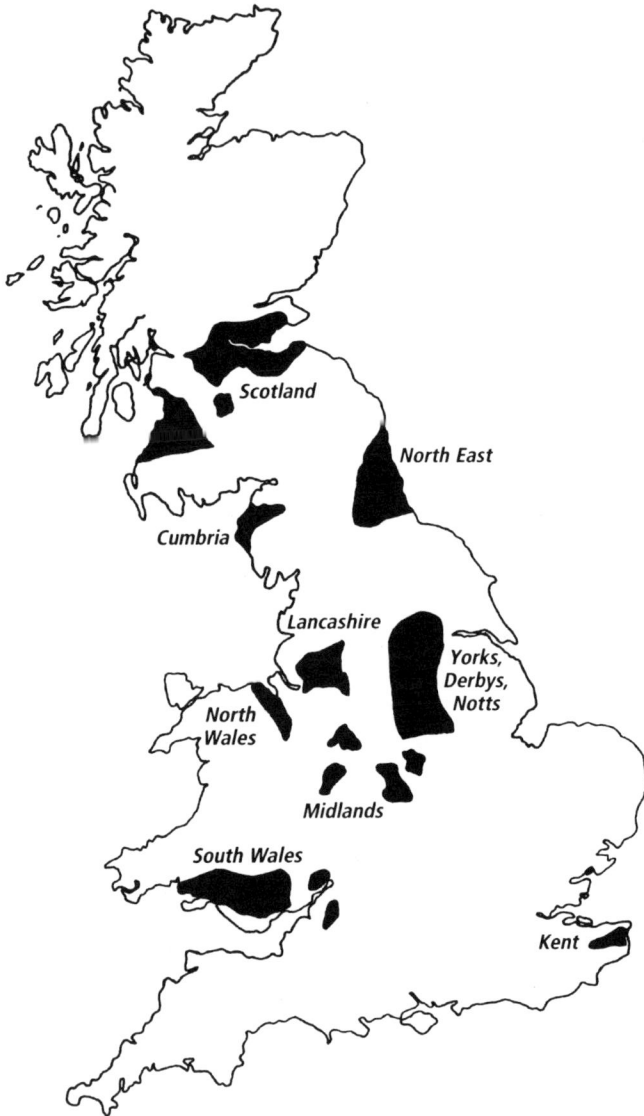

Scotland

North East

Cumbria

Lancashire

Yorks,
Derbys,
Notts

North
Wales

Midlands

South Wales

Kent

Contents

Prefatory Note

Late in 1996, Ludivina Garcia Arias, MEP, the Chairman of EURACOM, which represents all the West European coalfield communities, invited me to submit a report on unemployment in the coalfields. During the previous two years, I had presented extensive reports to the European Parliament on an action plan on employment policy, and on a coherent employment strategy for the European Union. These reports, together with the supplementary argumentation involved in preparing them, are published in a companion format to this little book, under the title *Full Employment for Europe*.*

Mrs Garcia Arias felt that the coalfields were indeed a special case needing detailed treatment. Pressure of other work unfortunately made it impossible for me to consider the situation in other European countries, although it is vitally necessary that the experiences of these countries should all be compared and contrasted with our own. I solicited help from Michael Barratt Brown, who has been a consistent source of wise counsel and active encouragement during all my work on the problem of unemployment. He readily agreed to join me in the preparation of this Report, which is in every particular a joint labour.

Three other participants in the project deserve the warmest thanks. They are my assistants in the coalfield constituency of North Nottinghamshire and Chesterfield. Ken Fleet has become an expert on the intricacies of European funding; Tony Simpson has devoted himself to tracking and understanding the complexities of environmental legislation in Europe and at home; and our troubleshooter, John Powell, has brought us more problems than all of us have been able to solve. Without their consistent advice and help, this book would have contained many more mistakes than it does.

Ken Coates MEP

---

*Ken Coates and Stuart Holland: *Full Employment for Europe*, Spokesman Books, 1995.

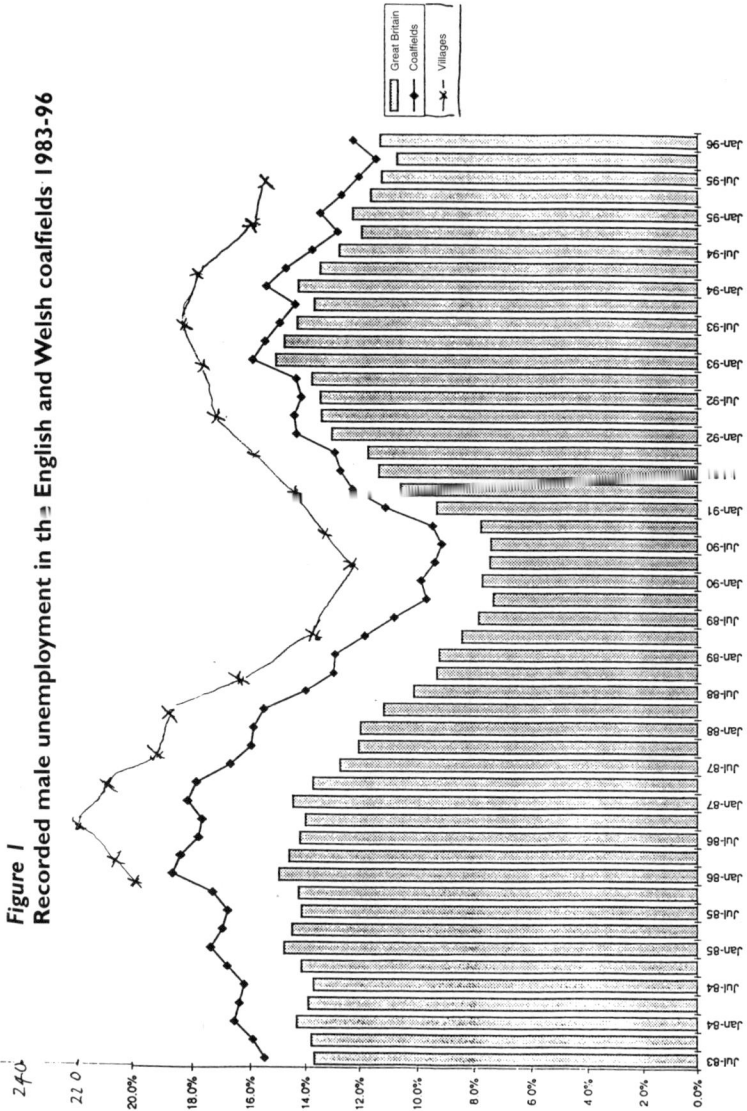

Figure I
Recorded male unemployment in the English and Welsh coalfields 1983-96

Legend:
Great Britain
Coalfields
Villages

Foreword

by Ludivina Garcia Arias MEP,
President of EURACOM

During recent years we in the European Parliament have known Ken Coates fighting for human rights and employment in Europe.

The political work in the European institutions may sometimes seem distant to some citizens from the concrete and daily issues, but in the case of Mr Coates' work one has the feeling that his commitment for these general issues is always related to actual citizens or groups of people suffering poverty, unemployment or human rights abuses.

The British coal industry, once the largest and one of the most competitive in the world, produced approximately half of the European Union's coal output. Absurdly, it has been reduced to almost nothing.

Sometimes the large figures tend to hide the human realities behind the decline of an economic activity or industry. But the figure of 200,000 mining jobs lost without pity in the United Kingdom in the decade from 1984, of which 80,000 were concentrated in the four years 1990-94, is startling when one thinks that it has happened in a handful of counties with a population of five million people.

The pages that follow have a great interest for the public in general and for other European coalfield areas where, in spite of different cultures and languages, there seems to exist a similar coalfield culture, built over generations of miners working underground and the mining industry structure and labour organisation.

Mr Coates describes brilliantly the consequences of the monopoly employment conditions planned by industries and active governmental intervention in the past which heavily jeopardise the economic recovery of these areas. He recalls that in the United Kingdom, and we can confirm that it happened elsewhere, 'competition for labour was actively stifled by preventing economic diversification ... on the grounds that the preservation of a near labour monopoly was essential to the survival of the coal industry, which was a national priority ...'.

He is correct when he affirms that 'the close specialisations within the mining industry generated particular skills which were not widely needed outside it, so that unemployed miners frequently found that only unskilled employment was open to them once they had been excluded from the pits' and that the absence of compensating employment for women in large parts of the coalfields had exacerbated an already harsh situation.

It is also true for the rest of Europe that the mining culture has many positive and transferable aspects: the traditional sense of community and the tradition of self-education among coal miners, which prepared many of them through institutions for adapting to a change in occupation when the decline in their industry accelerated; 'hard work for a fair reward, belief in the importance of social and economic justice, family and community values, comradeship and team working'. But there are also negative aspects like reluctance to accept retraining and education, belief in the inevitability of failure outside mining employment, insistence on retaining gender stereotypical roles and reluctance to train for work in 'non macho' occupations.

This cultural and sociological analysis is completed by Mr Coates when he establishes clearly the present association between unemployment and poverty, not only for the redundant miners and their families but also for the local economy.

Hope appears nevertheless when the author tells us about the efforts of local people to overcome these difficulties in spite of the lack of support from other national authorities.

Many pages describe excellent examples of great interest for other coalfield communities in Europe, from self-help programmes, such as the East Durham Community Development Initiative which shows how to bring about social and cultural regeneration in former coalfield areas, drawing local people into morale building activity and setting up local community organisations, or the Coalfields Learning Project based on South Yorkshire or the Fast Forward programme in Nottinghamshire.

What has happened in the British coalfield areas after 1984 cannot be extended to other Western European countries, where there has been a stronger commitment of central governments, regional bodies and, in some cases, the mining companies, for the economic recovery of the coalfield communities.

Nevertheless, the contents of Mr Coates' book are of great interest for the projects of coal reconversion in the Central and Eastern European areas where Mrs Thatcher's market model is often shown as a good mirror, hiding the real drama of the social consequences. For the rest of us, European coalfield communities, the good examples to follow, described in these pages, are the admirable efforts of self-help, lead by the Coalfield Communities Campaign (CCC), the local authorities, bodies and different citizens associations fighting against poverty, unemployment and environmental problems, showing all of us their practice and limitations but especially the strong will to survive and to offer their children a future.

As Ken Coates says: 'In spite of this adversity, a certain community sense lives on in most mining villages. This could form the basis for much grassroots self-help activity, showing high inventiveness and capacity'. Let us hope that the important political changes in the United Kingdom will compensate the historical debt with the British coalfield communities whose citizens contributed so much to their national economy and industry.

CHAPTER ONE

A Plea for the Coalfields Fourteen Years On

Tony Blair made his maiden speech in the House of Commons on the 6th July 1983, in the debate on the Finance Bill. As is customary, he spoke about the needs and problems of his Constituency. Sedgefield certainly had many problems, and Mr Blair set them in the context of the long and troubled history of the coalfield. His speech reflected the whole trauma of the brutal contraction of the coal industry in Durham. It was a powerful presentation. But he was not to know in mid-1983 that the story of the sufferings of the Durham mining communities would, within the decade, come to be shared by coalfield communities everywhere in the United Kingdom.

This is what Mr Blair said:

'I thank you, Mr Speaker, for allowing me this opportunity to make my maiden speech, especially on such an important Bill, as the new Member of Parliament for Sedgefield. I only hope that I can acquit myself as well as the Hon. Members who have preceded me in this difficult task.

Sedgefield is in County Durham, and having lived there for almost twenty years it was an especial honour for me to be chosen by the Labour Party to contest the seat. Given the Labour Party traditions of County Durham, my subsequent election with a good majority was hardly surprising, but it was no less pleasing to me for that.

The Constituency is remarkable for its variety and contrast. In the north-west is the large modern conurbation of Spennymoor, flanked by old mining villages, such as Chilton and Ferryhill. Turning east, one travels through more villages such as West Cornforth, Bishop Middleham, Trimdon Village, Trimdon Colliery and Fishburn, and still further east there are the villages of Wingate, Thornley, Wheatley Hill, Deaf Hill and Station Town. Although most of those villages share the common history of mining, they also have their own distinctive and separate character.

Sedgefield town itself is at the crux of the Constituency. It contains some new industry, the important hospital of Winterton and also has its prosperous residential parts. Travelling south from Sedgefield, one enters a different world altogether. One can tell that it is different because it is the place where the Social Democratic Party ceases telling the people that it represents the Labour Party of Attlee and Gaitskell and begins saying that it represents the Tory Party of Butler and Macmillan. Its towns include Hurworth, Middleton St. George, Whessoe and Heighington. It is sometimes suggested by the fainthearted that Labour support is less than solid here, but I have great faith in the good sense of the people.

This new Sedgefield Constituency is made up of parts of several other Constituencies, and I pay tribute to the Hon. Members from those parts – my Right Hon. Friend the Member for Durham, North-West (Mr Armstrong) and my Hon. Friends the Members for Easington (Mr Dorman), for Bishop Auckland (Mr Foster) and for City of Durham (Mr Hughes). I am grateful that they are all here as colleagues in this Parliament.

Though new in 1983, Sedgefield as a Constituency has in a sense only been in hibernation, as it existed as a Constituency until 1974. Distinguished predecessors have represented Sedgefield, the last three being John Leslie from 1935 to 1950, Joe Slater from 1950 to 1970 and David Reed from 1070 to 1974. Their maiden speeches provide an interesting synopsis of south-west Durham's history.

In the 1930s, John Leslie spoke of the poverty of his constituents, particularly the miners. However, in 1950, Joe Slater, himself a miner, described a better world where under public ownership

"the views of the miner are respected, and even acted upon, and that is how it ought to be". (*Official Report*, 29th March 1950; Vol. 473, c.489)

That was a speech of optimism. David Reed, who like me had the distinction of being the youngest Member of the Parliamentary Labour Party, also spoke with some optimism. He pointed out that the mining pits had largely closed but said:

"The influx of new industry into my Constituency has shown a remarkable increase during the last five years." (*Official Report*, 7th July 1970; Vol. 803, c.530)

In my maiden speech, I would have hoped to continue the theme of progress and optimism, but it is with the profoundest regret and not a little anger that I must say frankly that I cannot do so.

The speech most appropriate to my Constituency now is not the speech made in 1970 or even the speech made in 1950, but the speech that John Leslie made in the 1930s. In that speech, he said:

"Everyone will agree that it is nothing short of a tragedy that thousands of children are thrown on to the labour market every year with no possible prospect of continuous employment, with the result that thousands drift into blind alley jobs and drift out again. They have no proper training, they feel that they are not wanted and the future seems hopeless." (*Official Report*, 4th December 1935, Vol. 307, c.213)

That is tragically true for my Constituency today. In the area of the

Wingate employment exchange, which covers a very large part of the Constituency, unemployment now stands at over forty per cent. A large proportion of the unemployed are under twenty-five years of age. It is said with bitter irony that the only growth area in the Constituency is the unemployment office. Those young people are not merely faced with a temporary inability to find work. For many, the dole queue is their first experience of adult life. For some, it will be their most significant experience. Without work, they do not merely suffer the indignity of enforced idleness – they wonder how they can afford to get married, to start a family, and to have access to all the benefits of society that they should be able to take for granted. Leisure is not something that they enjoy, but something that imprisons them.

The Bill offers no comfort at all either to those people or to the vast majority of those of my constituents who are fortunate enough to be in work. Indeed, it adds the insult of inequality to the injury of poverty. It gives a further clutch of tax concessions to those who are already well off. Some 200,000 people are taken out of the higher rate bands, whereas only 10,000 come out of the poverty trap. That is a good illustration of the sense of priority shown in the Bill.

When I say "well off" I mean very well off. It is not those who earn the average wage who have benefited from the Government's fiscal policy, or even those who earn double the average. The only beneficiaries are those who earn more than three times the average. It is to that tiny and rarefied constituency that the Conservatives address themselves. The provisions of the Bill contradict in practical terms the myth that the Conservative Party is the Party of lower taxation for the people. In reality, lower taxation under the Conservative Administration has been confined to an exclusive club of the very privileged.

You may wonder, Mr Speaker, why, contrary to tradition, some maiden speeches have been controversial. Perhaps it is pertinent to ask in what sense they can be controversial, since the deprivation and unhappiness that afflict our constituencies seem beyond argument. What impels us to speak our minds is the sense of urgency. As I said, in the Wingate area, unemployment is over forty per cent. A Government who are complacent or uncaring about a level of unemployment of over forty per cent are a Government who have abdicated their responsibility to govern. A Government who refuse to govern are unworthy of the name of Government.

Yet despite the forty per cent unemployment, NSF, a subsidiary of the National Coal Board, announced in February this year a proposal to close the Fishburn coke works. If implemented, that proposal would push unemployment in the Wingate employment exchange area to over fifty per cent. The coke works is the major employer in Fishburn. It is not ailing. It is a highly efficient plant which produces some of the best domestic coke in the world. It provides work indirectly for many other people in the area, such as road hauliers and dockers.

In case anyone is unmoved by the loss of jobs, I can add that even in economic terms the closure is questionable. We are told that the recession is ending. I entirely agree with the Hon. Member for Loughborough (Mr Dorrell) that we need a broad-based economic recovery. My constituents are not interested in promises about economic recovery, they are interested in performance. In the recession, NSF loses money. However, the direct cost of closure in terms of redundancy payments, lost taxes and other related costs, amount to £3 million in the first year, and £1 million in the following years. To close Fishburn is an act of economic madness multiplied by social disregard on an unbelievable scale. Its only true justification is a blind allegiance to dogma.

Fishburn is significant not just in itself but as an example of the peril facing the north-east – a peril exemplified in the Bill. Fishburn is a real community. The Constituency of Sedgefield is made up of such communities. The local Labour Party grows out of, and is part of, local life. That is its strength. That is why my constituents are singularly unimpressed when told that the Labour Party is extreme. They see extremism more as an import from outside that is destroying their livelihoods than as a characteristic of the Party that is defending those livelihoods.

There is not a pit left in my Constituency. In the 1960s and the early 1970s new industry came to the Constituency but it often lacked strong roots. When the recession began to bite, many companies – particularly the multinationals – saw their northern outlets as the ones to be cut. Some still remain, including Thorns and Black and Decker, although both have suffered cutbacks. Carreras Rothman, also in Spennymoor, is one area of growth, but in general terms the picture is bleak. It should not be so because any discerning observer can see the advantages that the area offers. There is a capable and willing work force. There are massive amounts of factory space let at low rents by a District Council that, unlike central Government, is eager to assist economic growth. There is ready access by road, rail and air, and some of the most beautiful countryside in Britain.

What Sedgefield and the north-east desperately need is a Government committed to marrying together the resources of the area – a Government committed to the north. Over the last few years the level of investment in manufacturing industry in the north has dropped not merely in absolute terms but relative to other parts of the country. That situation must be reversed. In practical terms, the Government must pledge themselves to a massive investment in the region and must plan that investment.

I and others will continue to press for a northern development agency to perform for the north the task that the Scottish Development Agency performs for Scotland. That is not a request for fresh bureaucracy but a realistic assessment of need. Experience of the present Government may teach caution in hoping for such a commitment, but a refusal does not make the case for such a body any less strong. The aim would be to harness the considerable resources of the Constituency and the region and to let them work to create a better standard of living for the people. After all, that is the essence of Socialism.

I am a Socialist not through reading a textbook that has caught my intellectual fancy, nor through unthinking tradition, but because I believe that, at its best, Socialism corresponds most closely to an existence that is both rational and moral. It stands for co-operation, not confrontation, for fellowship, not fear. It stands for equality, not because it wants people to be the same but because only through equality in our economic circumstances can our individuality develop properly. British democracy rests ultimately on the shared perception by all the people that they participate in the benefits of the common weal. This Bill, with its celebration of inequality, is destructive of that perception. It is because of a fear that the Government seem indifferent to such considerations that I and my colleagues oppose the Bill and will continue to oppose it.'

Back in 1983 it was perfectly normal for a young Labour Parliamentarian to think in these terms. Mass unemployment called for Government action. Lack of investment called for Government action. The planning of resource use called for Government action, and so did the establishment of appropriate development agencies, not to enlarge bureaucracy, but to meet present needs. Such agencies would aim 'to harness the considerable resources ... to create a better standard of living for the people'.

In those far off days, such action was understood to be 'the essence of socialism'.

Equally, the politics of inequality were, in those days, unacceptable. Tax concessions to the wealthy were immediately and rightly weighted against conditions in the poverty trap. All this was a consensual reaction on the left, which saw the redistribution of income as part of a consistent strategy of redevelopment. Redistribution worked on at least three related levels. It worked on the dimension of class, transferring income from the rich to the poor. It also worked on the dimension of region, aiding development in the stricken zones by shifting resources from the more prosperous ones. And in the context of our argument it played a major role at the sectoral level, helping the people who had been working in declining sectors of the economy to readjust through the economic expansion of new growth industries.

What was true of the Durham coalfield in 1983 now applies with fearful force to vast areas of the York, Derby and Notts coalfields, and all the other devastated coalfield zones. Many of us think that redistribution, intervention and development remain the surest paths to recovery.

CHAPTER TWO

Community under Attack

Those who managed the exploitation of the coalfields of Britain have tipped many thousands of their workpeople out of work, and out of any reasonable prospect of work. They have not made any advance plans to create alternative occupations for those involved. This disaster has not been a small one. The British coal industry, once the largest in the world, has in the last decade suffered the sharpest contraction of output of any European coal or other industry. From producing approximately half of the European Union's coal output, its contribution has been reduced to less than a third of a diminishing overall total: and continuing further reductions are highly likely. Yet apart from assistance to the coal producing companies with their restructuring (including redundancy payments to dismissed miners), the original intentions of the European Coal and Steel Community have been largely disregarded.

Articles 46 and 56(2) of the Treaty of Paris provided for extensive measures to help the workers in the industrial redevelopment of areas of pit closure. But the interventionist assumptions of Jean Monnet, like his Federal commitments, have been corroded over time, and it is nowadays assumed that enhanced severance payments are enough to send the coal industry's employees on their way, to nowhere in particular, to find whatever jobs there may, or may not, be.

What has not been done under the terms of the ECSC Treaty has, it is true, been partly attempted by European Regional Funds. And there remains always a great gap which can only be filled by action on the part of the British Government, which, for years, intervened to keep miners captive in the pits by preventing alternative industrial development which might have offered them better jobs: but which

Table 1
Employment in British Coal 1981-97

	Total workforce* (thousands)	No. of miners (thousands)	No. of collieries
Sept. 1981	279.2	218.8	211
Sept. 1982	266.3	208.0	200
Sept. 1983 **	246.8	191.7	191
March 1985	21.3	171.4	169
March 1986	179.6	138.5	133
March 1987	141.5	107.7	110
March 1988	117.3	89.0	94
March 1989	105.0	80.1	86
March 1990	85.0	65.4	73
March 1991	73.3	57.3	65
March 1992	58.1	43.8	50
March 1993	44.2	31.7	50
March 1994	18.9	10.8	19
March 1995	c13.0	c10.0	c19
March 1996	c13.0	c10.0	c19
March 1997	c13.0	c10.0	19 (25)***

Source: British Coal Corporation, Annual Reports; Coalfield Communities' Campaign and *Energy Trends*.
* 'Workforce' until 1994 is for British Coal Corporation and after that for all employment in deep mines, of which RJB Mining owns 19.
** There are no figures for 1984, reflecting the shift from September to March as the recording date for British Coal's statistics.
*** Figure in brackets for collieries in 1997 is for all deep mined pits, including others than those of RJB Mining.

Table 1a
Employment in Deep Mines, July 1997

Company	Industrial Employees	Other employees	Sub-contractors	Totals	No. of Deep mines
RJB Mining	7,420	440	2,471	10,331	19
Midland Mining	752	102	236	1,090	2
Scottish Coal	701	163	230	1,094	1
Hatfield Coal Co. Ltd.	159	19	35	213	1
Tower Anthracite*	170	15	30	215	1
Betws Anthracite*	80	8	0	88	1
Totals	9,282	747	3,002	13,031	25

*Figures for Tower and Betws are estimates. The rest were submitted by companies in July 1997. Coalfield Communities' Campaign.

now declines to intervene, and hides behind the fiction that the recovery of employment for its victims can simply be left to the workings of the market.

But it is not thanks to the market that our coalfields came to depend on a single industry for men's work: the competition for labour was actively stifled by preventing economic diversification.

Employment in the British mining industry was reduced by 200,000 in the decade from 1984. 80,000 of these job losses were concentrated in the four years 1990-94. (Table 1 and 1A above.) The whole industry had always been concentrated, crowded into counties with a population of 5 million out of the UK total of 55 million. These were Durham, South Yorkshire, Derbyshire and Nottinghamshire, Mid-Glamorgan, Fife and Ayrshire.

These UK Coalfield areas had for several decades suffered higher unemployment than the rest of the country, but it appears that in the years of economic growth up to 1990, the unemployed men were

Table 2

National and Coalfield Unemployment, Great Britain, 1990-96

Region/County	Unemployment Rates (%) January of					Difference from national (%)				
	1990	1992	1993	1995	1996	1990	1992	1993	1995	1996
United Kingdom	..	9.4	8.9	8.2	8.0	..	..	..	..	..
North	9.1	11.2	11.8	11.3	10.2	3.2	2.8	2.9	3.1	2.2
Durham	8.6	11.1	11.6	10.0	n.a.	2.7	1.7	2.7	1.8	n.a.
Northumberland	7.8	10.3	10.8	11.1	n.a.	1.9	0.9	1.9	1.9	n.a.
Yorks/H'berside	7.2	9.7	9.9	9.2	8.5	1.3	0.3	1.0	1.0	0.5
S. Yorks	9.8	12.6	12.6	12.0	n.a.	3.9	3.2	3.7	2.8	n.a.
East Midlands	5.1	8.7	9.8	8.4	7.4	-0.8	0.7	0.7	0.2	-0.6
Derbyshire	5.5	9.1	9.3	9.1	8.0	0.4	0.3	0.4	0.9	0.0
Notts	6.6	10.0	10.5	10.3	10.4	0.7	0.6	1.6	2.1	2.4
Wales	6.8	9.9	10.4	9.2	8.2	0.9	0.5	1.5	1.0	0.2
Mid-Glamorgan	8.7	12.4	12.0	10.8	n.a.	2.8	3.0	3.1	2.6	n.a.
Scotland	8.7	9.7	9.9	9.0	8.0	2.8	0.3	1.0	0.8	0.0
Fife	9.2	10.9	11.0	11.2	n.a.	3.3	1.5	2.1	3.0	n.a.

Note: There were changes in definition of unemployment rates after 1992. All differences shown are percentage points *plus*, unless a minus sign is shown.

Sources: Regions/counties 1990-95 from *Regional Trends*, 1990-1995 editions. 1996 figures for Regions from *Economic Trends*, November 1996. Counties from Derbyshire and Notts County Councils' respective *Monthly Unemployment Statistics*.

absorbed into the economy and the gap between coalfield rates of male unemployment and the national average actually narrowed (see fig. 1 above from Beatty and Fothergill). After 1991 the coalfields/national gap stabilised, but the gap between rates for the pit villages themselves and the national average widened again. The effect on the overall (men's and women's) rates was to maintain and even widen the gap between coalfield areas and the national average unemployment rate. (Table 2).

There appears to have been little or no improvement since in the relative unemployment rates in the coalfield counties, least of all in the actual coalfield districts. (See Table 2, and Table 3 in Chapter 4.)

The economic cost to the coalfield areas over a single decade can be roughly calculated. The loss of 200,000 jobs which had earned each worker an average wage of £400 a week or £20,000 a year, amounts overall to a direct loss of income of £4,000 million. Assuming generously that these men and their families continued to receive half that amount, either from new jobs or from state benefit, then the loss of individual earnings to the areas concerned would be some £2,000 million. Taking into account the loss of income from local supplies to the industry and the consequent multiplier effect, the net loss in one year will not have been less than £4,000 million from an income of the coalfield areas in 1991 of about £50,000 million, i.e. a loss of about 8%.

British economic history can show few examples of such a concentrated shock to the economy as this was. Certainly, throughout the post-war years, only the initial problem of demobilisation posed more serious problems to the economic planners than those which have arisen in the destruction of the mining industry.

After the Second World War, Britain had to redeploy a very large army from the battle fronts, and to arrange for the transfer from military to civilian production of an immense arms industry. Between mid-1945 and mid-1947, 3,800,000 men and women left the armed services, and over a period of two years longer, the munitions industry was to redeploy nearly four and a half million people. Working for success were the facts that domestic demand had been squeezed to the bone throughout the years of wartime austerity, so that almost any consumer products could be sold; that there was a backlog of six years' neglect in many sectors of the economy: and the fact that overseas markets were temporarily almost infinite, since so much destruction had been wrought on all the European allies, and on the enemy nations as well. Even the exhausted British firms, labouring with obsolescent equipment, and archaic methods of work organisation, could sell into these markets, at any rate in the early postwar years. The result was a chronic labour shortage. But in addition, the British Government had resolved on macro-economic policies determined by J. M. Keynes and William Beveridge. Beveridge had presumed an unemployment rate no higher than three per cent. As late as June 1944, the Chancellor of the Exchequer sought to impose an 8.5 per cent limit to unemployment as a working assumption, but in the wartime coalition, this was not politically acceptable, and he was overruled.

In spite of various attempts to loosen the employment targets, particularly during crises such as the Korean War, employment policy remained remarkably constant over the next decades. Within this framework, various fiscal controls were combined with a planning regime, much criticised at the time, which ensured that the postwar years established and maintained virtually full employment, in spite of the vast difficulties involved in relocating so many servicemen and women, so many munitions workers. Compared with these traumas, the end of the coal industry should, surely, have been greatly more manageable.

But the displacement of our mineworkers took place at a different time, when sharply different orthodoxies were in force. Thatcher ruled, red in tooth and claw. 'Plan' had become a four letter word. That which the market could not secure unaided by Government action, ought better, it was felt, remain unthinkable. So macro-economic policy would not work for the coalfield communities, whoever else it served.

An interventionist regime would have taken the imminent collapse of coal mining very differently. It was an open invitation, first to change macro-economic policy, and second to develop precise planning instruments to deal with the detailed problems on the ground. We can find an apposite example about how this could have been done from Sweden.

When the Swedish Government was faced with the prospect of a rapid and significant reduction in their national ship building industry, they took very considerable measures to prepare the workers who would lose their jobs for new employment, not only by retraining programmes, but by investment in new enterprise. The Government ensured that the closures took place over a period of several years, that unemployment pay was maintained at a high level, that free training was available for those wishing to change or develop their skills, that subsidies in the form of interest-free loans were available to new firms coming into the area, and that all employers knew of the resources available for converting production out of shipbuilding. (see Frank Blackaby, 'Conversion and Industrial Change', *ENDpapers*, No. 20, Autumn 1989.)

The British miners were not to benefit from this Scandinavian experience. Instead, they were to suffer the full rigour of Governmental inaction and indifference.

The official figures of unemployment can be shown to underestimate the real numbers without work everywhere, but especially in the coalfield areas. This is because some miners were registered as permanently sick after their redundancy, while others received large enough redundancy payments to deprive them of benefit. So neither of these categories, nor that of men and women temporarily on short courses of training, are counted as claimants seeking work, which is the current definition of the unemployed. The score of those men who have obtained work and the women who have taken up work to supplement the family income can be shown to be less than half of the total of those of working age.

Those men and women who have found work after pit closures are, moreover, frequently paid at very low rates. There is much dismal evidence about this. One former miner at Ollerton colliery told us of his joy at winning a job after extensive interviews had rejected numbers of other applicants, and then of his dismay when he learned that his new *weekly* wage would hardly exceed the *daily* rate he had been paid while he worked in the pit. Another former Union branch official, at Bolsover, told us how his new employment as a night watchman pays him an unvarying sum of £2 an hour, while he works all Bank Holidays, including Christmas Day, Boxing Day and New Year's Day, without respite.

The loss to those individuals has been crushing. But the loss to the local economy has evidently been even greater than appears. It can be estimated that whether finding new work or not, miners' household expenditure is halved in relation to what it was. Poverty, as officially defined at half the average household income, is widespread among the unemployed miners and their families.

In spite of this adversity, a certain community sense lives on in most mining villages. This could form the basis for regeneration, and there is already much grassroots self-help activity, showing high inventiveness and capacity. A very wide range of projects has been proposed for support by those funds which are available locally, nationally and from the European Union. These include many schemes for the education and training of redundant mineworkers, whose now redundant skills are often not easily adapted to work outside the mines. Only a very small proportion of the projects proposed, however, have received funding and many more projects for offering necessary conservation and environmental and other useful work to unemployed men and women in the coalfields rest in files in local authority offices.

The actual net loss to the economy of the coalfields from the pit closure programme we have reckoned at some £4 billion. Against this the sums received so far have been very considerably smaller. Two Rechar programmes have brought £275 million from the European Community. Rather more has come from European Regional Development Funds under their Objective 2. Something rather less than this has come from UK sources. Michael Heseltine's government promise to contribute £1000 million included enhanced redundancy settlements in the net loss figure given above, and a significant part of these payments came from the programmes of the European Coal and Steel Community. Payments through local authorities were much lower than had at first been assumed.

Long term unemployment, and the sustained waste of the talent of the young generation, are still rife throughout the coalfields, which urgently need new investment in both infrastructure and new economic capacity, if they are to be reclaimed from the wilderness.

This is the more necessary because the prospects for the British coal industry, as for other European coal industries, are not rosy. According to current predictions, demand for British coal is set to fall from 55 million tonnes in 1996 to 35 million tonnes in 2001. This could mean nearly halving the present already greatly reduced number of mining jobs in the coalfield areas, mainly now in Yorkshire and the East Midlands. But current predictions are undergoing frenzied revisions, with the continued expansion of gas-fired power generation, and with new discoveries of large gas reserves in the North Sea.

CHAPTER THREE

How Coal Came to Dominate

T he decline of the British coal industry has been going on for a very long time, even though this decline accelerated in the 1980s. For the first quarter of this century there were never less than a million men employed in the industry. In 1921 this was 9 per cent of all employees in Britain and the industry still accounted in 1931 for 7.3 per cent of the employed population. By 1951 the proportion had fallen to 4.3 per cent and this was halved by the end of the 1970s. But it still represented 280,000 men. Today the total employed in the industry is about 13,000, no more than 10,000 of whom are actually coal miners.

The UK regions in which the coalfields are found are, moreover, mainly those where other industries have also been declining – shipbuilding, steel making, heavy engineering and agriculture. Only in the West Midlands and East Midlands and in some parts of Scotland has there been a significant inflow of investment in new industries to replace the old. Even there, new projects have normally been kept separate from colliery settlements, at least until the pits themselves have closed. And very recently the Midlands, too, have been losing job opportunities. The North of England, Yorkshire, Lancashire, Derbyshire, Wales and large parts of Scotland have been in almost continuous decline for seventy years, and these regions include most of the British coalfields.

Concentrations of Employment

There is a further special characteristic of coalfields: very frequently the pattern of settlement in them spreads across a large number of small mining villages, surrounded by agricultural land. In the nineteenth century, such villages commonly had little or no public transport facilities, so that mining employment was conditioned by the distance involved in walking to work. Mines that were sunk in the twentieth century could commonly call on labour from a much wider catchment, so that in North Derbyshire and more particularly in Nottinghamshire, mining towns such as Mansfield or Worksop, Nottingham or Chesterfield could furnish labour to a large number of collieries surrounding them. Such collieries would originally be the focus of active bus routes, and later would require large car parks, as the miners became independently mobile.

Where the predominant pattern of settlement was in mining villages, pit wages could fall below the national average. But if there were some alternative employment possibilities, as in the vicinity of Leicester, Nottingham, Staffordshire and Kent, then there could be a marked appreciation in wage levels. The absence of alternative employment opportunities elsewhere did not happen by chance.

Even in the mining towns of these areas, there were constant and repetitive pressures from mine workers for the diversification of the local economy, in order to enable young men to escape the inevitability of employment in coal mining. Successive governments of different political persuasions, however, became continuously engaged in the discouragement of planning for job diversification, on the grounds that the preservation of a near labour monopoly was essential to the survival of the coal industry, which was a national economic priority. A typical example of this kind of intervention is to be found in the West Nottinghamshire Town Map prepared in 1963 in accordance with the provisions of the *Town and Country Planning Act 1962*.* This records:

> 'The approved Development Plan was concerned with the marked dependence of the area on coal mining, particularly the problems likely to arise from the release of labour and capital when the coal seams could no longer be economically worked. "One of the County's chief industrial problems is the introduction of alternative male employment into the coalfield districts which might be considered desirable to give stability to the industrial structure." (County Report of Survey, Volume III.) The Board of Trade's view was however that no large measure of alternative male employing industry was desirable in a coalfield area with an existing manpower shortage. Equally the Board was more sympathetic to steering female employing projects to coal mining settlements where female employment is lacking or available only at the expense of considerable daily

*West Nottinghamshire Town Map 1968-1981, p.21

travel. In 1951, the major problem was a shortage of labour, both female and juvenile. The local Planning Authority held the view that the coal industry was unlikely to expand its labour requirements, and in fact there has been little change in colliery manpower."

Mining is, indeed, an industry worked almost entirely by men. The planners were right to insist that women's work is sometimes hard to come by in a coalfield locality and is for the reasons just explained not likely to be available except at some distance from the mines.

Mining is not an unskilled occupation: on the contrary. But apart from the work of electrical and engineering craftsmen, the skills required are highly specific to mining. Originally, at the turn of the century, they were learnt by instruction from father to son. Commonly colliers then had only a minimum of book learning, which was even somewhat despised among them. The development of longwall mining, loading coal onto long conveyor belts, running the length of a coal-face for perhaps one hundred yards or more, put an end to the stall system, in which a small group of men would work together in a small heading, sharing all the tasks of winning the coal, packing the sides of the workings with waste rock, and supporting the roof with props. Longwall working also ultimately broke the butty system of payment via the headman of a gang with its frequent associated dependence on close family ties. No longer could a father engage and employ his sons in a closed team. With large numbers of face workers engaged in a range of distinct tasks, mechanization became more and more possible, and more and more necessary. The mechanization involved the acquisition of important mechanical skills, and effected considerable changes in the necessary formal educational attainments of the workforce.

Within two decades after the Second World War, miners were becoming much more literate and numerate, and training within the coal industry both encouraged and ministered to this development. Nonetheless, the close specializations within the mining industry generated particular skills which were not widely needed outside it, so that unemployed miners frequently found that only unskilled employment was open to them once they had been excluded from the pits. And it is, of course, the case that demand for such unskilled work has been steadily declining for some seventy years, even in the construction industry.

The most recent sharp diminution of the coal industry, with

employment reduced to less than a tenth in a decade, has struck at an industry that was already in decline, situated largely in areas with little or no local alternative job opportunities. The absence of compensating employment for women in large parts of the coalfields has exacerbated an already harsh situation. It will be no surprise to find that household incomes in the coalfields are from 15 to 20 per cent below the national average, which means that they may be as little as a half of those in more affluent areas.

All this was known to the authorities, and particularly well known to Local Authorities. But in spite of the repeated warnings of councillors and trade unions, the pit closure programme of the late nineteen eighties was driven through without pity, and without any trace of effective measures to mitigate its dreadful consequences.

CHAPTER FOUR

Unemployment in
the British Coalfields

The Destruction of the Coal Industry

The scale of the reduction in employment in the UK coal industry between 1981 and 1994 exceeds any similar employment change in the United Kingdom or in continental Europe. A workforce of 279,000 was reduced to one of 13,000, numbers of coal miners from 219,000 to about 10,000 and the number of pits from 211 to 25. This reduction took place moreover in only 18 counties out of the UK's 68, with a population of around five million out of a UK population of 55 million in 1981. The coal industry provided about a quarter of all the male jobs located in the coalfield areas. Most were concentrated in pit settlements which comprised about a third of the coalfield areas' population, but included two thirds of all the jobs in coal mining. In these areas coal provided as much as half of all the jobs. Given the long years of decline, commuting out of the pit villages for work was already well established, but the location of these villages set limits to such commuting.

In view of the past history of the coalfields, and the most recent melt-down of the industry,* it is inevitable that unemployment rates should be higher in the coalfields than elsewhere in the UK. Table 3 shows that most are indeed two or three percentage points above the national average.

What is, however, most surprising, and has caught the attention of those making statistical studies, is that the gap between the coalfields

---

*People speak about this as a 'decimation'. But when the Roman legions were culled, one man in ten stepped forward for execution. The attack on the coalmining industry carried off nine men out of ten.

Table 3
Coalfield Profiles 1994

Region, County or District	Household Income, per head % of UK	Activity Rates				Unemployed Claimants of which (%)			At School over 16 (%)
		All	Male	Female All	p/t	rate	female	long tm	
UK	100	62.2	73.7	52.5	24.7	8.9	23.4	37.0	80
North	91.1	58.9	70.1	49.7	24.3	11.3	19.8	36.3	71
Durham	85.1	58.8				10.0	19.0	29.8	70
Yorks/H'berside	92.5	61.3	73.2	51.3	25.6	9.4	22.1	34.7	74
S.Yorks	86.7	55.7				12.0	20.6	37.5	68
Barnsley		51.2					18.8	32.2	
East Midlands	94.7	62.8	75.2	53.7	25.8	8.4	23.5	35.4	76
Derbyshire	88.7	63.3				9.0	22.1	35.3	75
Erewash		58.1					22.2	33.8	
Notts	92.7	60.0				10.3	21.7	39.7	73
Mansfield		57.5					19.9	36.4	
West Midlands	93.0	62.9	75.5	52.6	25.8	8.8	23.9	40.8	76
Staffs	95	63.0				7.5	29.4	32.5	74
Wales	88.8	56.9	69.0	48.5	23.3	9.2	22.2	34.3	68
Mid-Glamorgan	79.7	54.4				10.8	19.7	35.8	76
Scotland	99.0	62.3	72.1	51.4	23.1	9.0	22.5	33.2	83
Fife	97.3	64.0				11.2	22.4	33.0	100

Source: CSO *Regional Trends*, No.30, 1995 edition.

rates and the national average far from widening in the last decade has actually narrowed. The question that has had to be answered is: what has happened to all those almost a quarter of a million men who have lost their jobs in the coal industry in the last decade? As Table 3 shows, economic activity rates in the coalfields areas do not appear to be so very much lower – for men or for women – or unemployment so very much higher than in other areas.

Hidden Unemployment

The answer to this conundrum has been discovered in the Sheffield Hallam University studies of 'Registered and Hidden Unemployment in the UK Coalfields', by Beatty and Fothergill. These studies took the period covered by the two censuses of 1981 and 1991, during which some three-quarters of job losses to date had already occurred in the coal industry. The authors added to the job losses a figure for natural increases in the labour force and then looked for those who could be

accounted for under five headings:
1. net out migration
2. increase in net out-commuting
3. reduction in labour force participation
4. increase in jobs in other industries
5. take up into government training schemes.

They applied this search first to the coalfield areas and then to the actual coalfield villages, with the following results. Out of one hundred 'surplus' male workers resulting from loss of coal jobs and natural increase in the workforce, the destinations were as shown in Table 4.

Table 4
Destination of 'Surplus' Coalfield Labour, GB 1981-91 (%)

Destination	From Coalfields Areas	From Pit Villages
1. Migration	27	28
2. Dropped out	38	25
3. Other employment	20	17
4. Extra commuters	2	16
5. Government schemes	12	8
Total	99	94
Extra unemployed	..	6

Source: Christina Beatty and Stephen Fothergill, *Registered and Hidden Unemployment in the UK Coalfields*, Sheffield Hallam University, 1996.

The key figures in the Table for understanding what is really hidden unemployment are those for the reduction in labour force participation (shown as 'dropped out'). For women such a figure would imply the lack of job availabilies and the demands of household work. For men the main reasons, apart from disappearance into the black economy, are permanent sickness and early retirement, either official or voluntary, given the lack of job prospects for those with only a few years to go until their 65th birthday. Recorded rates of permanent sickness doubled in the coalfield areas between 1981 and 1991. Rates of permanent sickness in the coalfields were then found to be between two and a half and three times higher than those in the South East of England. This is partly the result of coal mining risks, but also because sickness benefit was higher than other benefits and was often not an unreasonable claim to be made by older men after a lifetime underground.

31

The British Government's changing measure of unemployment for statistical purposes has been the subject of much criticism. The monthly figures are derived from those claiming unemployment-related benefits. This does not include the permanently sick or those with savings, redundancy payments or partner's earnings which would render them ineligible. A quite different basis of calculations has been adopted by Beatty and Fothergill in the Sheffield/Hallam study. This is to count those who 'might reasonably expect to work in a fully employed economy, whether or not they happen to be active job seekers'. On this count they estimate the real unemployment rate for the coalfields in 1991 to have been 22.5 per cent, or almost double the registered unemployed figure of 12.4 per cent. For the pit villages, the difference was between 26.7 per cent and 14 per cent. The most telling result of this calculation is that the Beatty and Fothergill system of counting raises the unemployment rate for the whole of the UK in 1991 only from 10.6 per cent to 14.9 per cent – not a doubling. So hidden unemployment is much greater in the coalfield areas than elsewhere. (The details for different coalfields are given in Table 5.)

Table 5
Alternative measures of pit village male unemployment, GB April 1991

| | Percentage of economically active males 16-64 | |
	DE registered unemployment	Real unemployment
Ayrshire	20.3	36.1
South Wales	16.7	33.3
Yorkshire	15.1	27.8
Northumberland	15.0	28.1
Durham	14.8	33.9
Fife/Central	13.5	21.8
Lothian	13.1	23.0
N. Derbyshire	12.5	23.6
Nottinghamshire	11.9	21.2
S Derbys/NW Leics	8.2	15.7
All pit villages	14.0	26.7
GB	10.6	14.9

Source: NOMIS, Census of Population, authors' estimates. Beatty & Fothergill.

A part of this difference is the result of the manner of counting and this is confirmed by the alternative method of calculation used in the studies by the Unemployment Unit. These simply continue the old

Figure 2
Male unemployment in 15 coalfield districts, January 1997

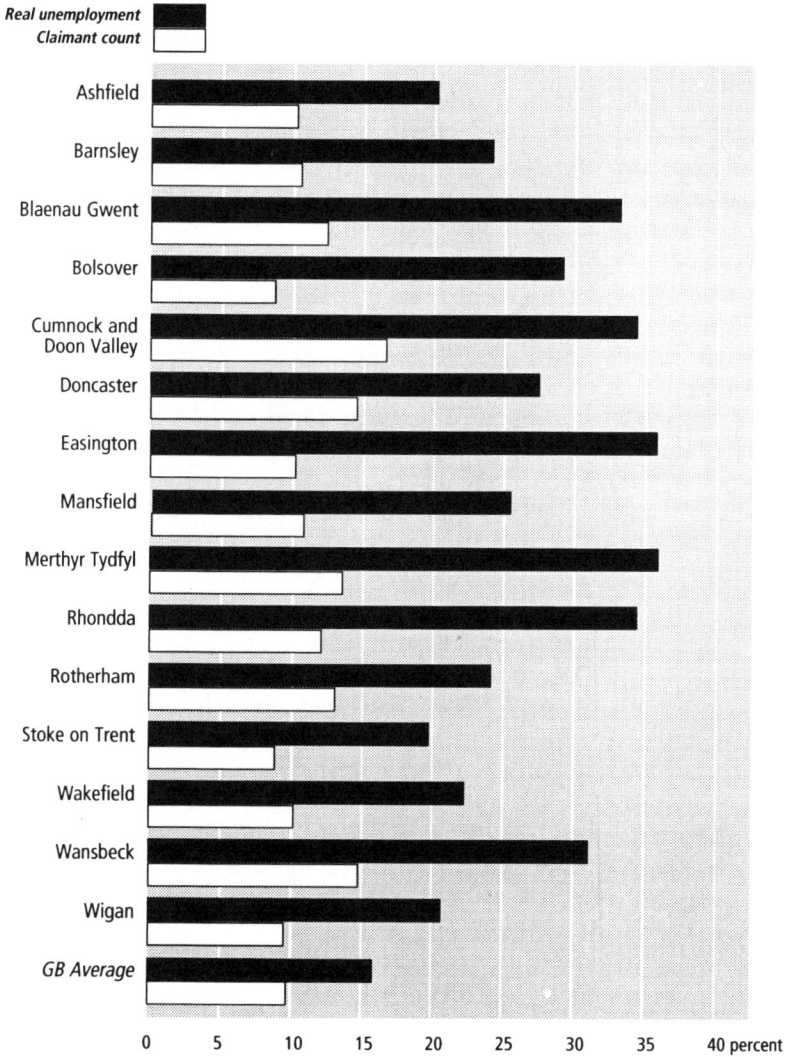

Real unemployment
Claimant count

Ashfield
Barnsley
Blaenau Gwent
Bolsover
Cumnock and Doon Valley
Doncaster
Easington
Mansfield
Merthyr Tydfyl
Rhondda
Rotherham
Stoke on Trent
Wakefield
Wansbeck
Wigan
GB Average

0   5   10   15   20   25   30   35   40 percent

Source: Sheffield Hallam University.

basis for counting before the Government made the twenty-eight successive changes between 1979 and 1995. While the official count in 1991 gave an unemployment rate for the whole of the UK of 10 per cent for men, the Unemployment Unit's figure was 14 per cent. But in addition there are other factors: permanent sickness, redundancy savings and temporary training courses, which each exclude large numbers from the count of unemployed. In three Derbyshire Coalfield districts in 1994 the difference between the official count and the Unemployment Unit figure was much wider than that for the UK as a whole – 11 per cent and 18 per cent, compared with 8.5 per cent and 12 per cent. This further confirms the Beatty-Fothergill assumption of a high level of hidden unemployment in the coalfield areas.

Further confirmation is available for certain pit villages. A house to house survey, described as a local skills audit, was made in 1995 for three pit villages in North Derbyshire: Shirebrook, Creswell, Langwith and Whaley Thorns (see Table 6). Over a half of the 7000 households visited completed a questionnaire that was delivered. This revealed even more startling results. While the official unemployment rates were recorded as about 20 per cent for men and 10 per cent for women, the survey found that just one half of the male respondents, between the ages of 16 and 64 and not at school, described themselves as unemployed and likewise more than half of the women between 16 and 59 years not at school. Very few men were working part-time and very few women had full-time employment, but one-third of the women were working part-time. Unemployment was as high among the young as among the old.

This question is worth examining further, in the light of the official proposals for dealing with youth unemployment. It is suggested that a key policy target must be to 'get people off welfare into work'. Hence we have the strategy of a windfall tax on the profits of public utilities, hypothecated to finance a 'welfare to work' programme. Critics have styled this 'Welfare to Workfare'.

Such a programme is based on the notion that long-term unemployment exists because there is a pool of supposedly 'unemployable' people, whose incapacities swell the numbers of the workless. But when a large proportion of the long-term unemployed are young, we are bound to ask how it comes about that unemployability is concentrated in particular areas.

Table 6
Shirebrook Skills Audit 1995 – Summary

Ward	Households visited no.	Quest'aires completed no.		Total persons no.	In Work Men %	In Work Women %	In School Over 16 no.	Fearful of future %
East	632	186	30	276	48	42	12	50
North	479	274	57	396	44	40	23	35
N/West	627	357	57	524	47	42	27	44
South	714	477	67	795	44	45	42	41
S/West	1143	681	59	1089	56	53	70	40
Scarc'lf E	867	360	41	629	53	35	28	49
Scarc'lf N	475	226	48	311	49	31	11	62
Creswell	2052	1074	53	1522	47	40	73	36
Totals	6989	3635	52	5542	49	43	286	43

Notes:
'Total persons' means all those in households for which questionnaires were returned.
'In work' includes full-time and part-time work.
'In school' includes all in education, a very few of whom were over 24.
'Fearful for future' means belief that the area faced decline.

Thanks to the work of David Webster in Glasgow, we can see that no such presumption is necessary, because the theory itself is quite untrue. So is the associated theory of 'withering flowers', which suggests that experience of long-term unemployment makes people less employable. The Treasury notion has been that people get to like living on benefits, and are reluctant to forego them. But benefits are fixed at painfully low levels, even if wages are nudging downwards against them in large parts of the coalfields.

What David Webster did was to examine the correlation between levels of total unemployment as a percentage of the labour force and levels of long term unemployment as a percentage of the same labour force. He found that there was a constant relationship. If unemployment rises, long-term unemployment rises with it. And both decline together. It is true that there is a proportion of the population with genuine handicaps, but these people are a very small number, and are not the subjects of the thinking which has given rise to 'welfare to work'. As Webster puts it:

'Long term unemployment has not been "ratcheted up" since the 1970s, but has come down in step with total unemployment exactly as it rose.'

Figure 3
Unemployment rates – GB, 1949-92. All unemployed and long-term unemployed*

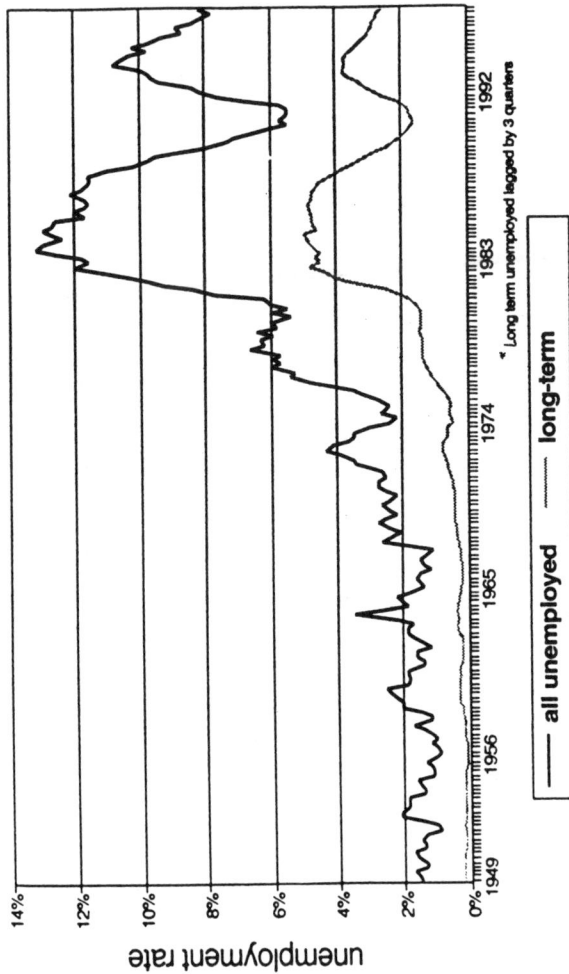

Source: Working Brief, No.85, June 1997.

Table 7
Unemployment:
North Nottinghamshire and North Eastern Derbyshire, 1995-7

	Numbers of Unemployed Claimants		
	April 1995	*April 1996*	*April 1997*
Four Nottinghamshire Parliamentary Constituencies			
A Total Claimant Count	16,162	14,317	10,512
B Long-term included (over 52 weeks)	5,779	4,919	3,343
B as a percent of **A**	35.8%	34.4%	31.8%
Three Derbyshire Parliamentary Constituencies			
A Total Claimant Count	12,208	10,875	8,230
B Long-term included (over 52 weeks)	4,696	3,898	2,916
B as percent of **A**	38.5%	35.84%	35.4%
Seven Constituencies together			
A Total Claimant Count	28,370	25,192	18,742
B Long-term included (over 52 weeks)	10,475	8,817	6,259
B as percent of **A**	36.9%	35%	33.4%

Notes: In all the above cases long-term unemployment is falling *faster* than overall unemployment.

The long-term unemployed are unemployed because there are no jobs. If jobs materialise, they will go to work. In the absence of jobs, non-interventionist governments seek to move the long-term unemployed around schemes which keep them off the streets, but which do not solve their problem.

Webster pursued his studies in Glasgow, where he is trying to help the City Council to cope with a prolonged shortage of jobs. In the decade between 1981 and 1991, Glasgow, like Manchester, lost 30 per cent of its blue collar jobs. Liverpool lost 40 per cent. The coalfields share a similar fate. Replacement jobs were slow to materialise, and it is this slowness, a result of deliberate social policy, which accounts for long-term unemployment, not individual fecklessness. Other important social problems also correlate with high long-term unemployment figures: the incidence of lone parenthood, for instance.

When we looked at the unemployment figures in North Nottinghamshire and North Eastern Derbyshire, we found a decided confirmation of Webster's view of this matter (see Table 7). Taking the four Nottinghamshire Parliamentary Constituencies which include the main part of the old Nottinghamshire coalfield, and the three North

Eastern Derbyshire Parliamentary Constituencies, which cover that part of the Derbyshire coalfield which had survived through to the late seventies, we find that in April 1996 the claimant unemployed numbered 25,192. By April 1997 there had been a decline in the unemployed numbers which had fallen to 18,742. The long-term unemployed had also declined, somewhat *faster* than the overall numbers of unemployed. In 1996, 35 per cent of the total claimant unemployed had been unemployed for more than one year. But the following year, the percentage had shrunk to 33.4 per cent. All this took place without the benefit of welfare to work, as new jobs became available.

CHAPTER FIVE

Unemployment and Poverty

The association between unemployment and poverty is obvious and well established since Seebohm Rowntree's surveys in York at the turn of the century, and again in the 1930s.

In the survey on poverty in the St Ann's district of Nottingham, in which one of the authors was involved through the second half of the '60s, we found that the contribution of unemployment to the generation of poverty had markedly diminished. The most numerous group of poor people were pensioners, and they were closely shadowed by the working low-paid. Then came lone parents, and, last of all, the sick. Unemployment accounted for 13 per cent of the poor. It has become much more evident once more in recent years, partly because of the increase in long-term unemployment, and in the unemployment of young people contributing to household incomes, and partly because of the decline in the value of unemployment benefit. This fell during the 1980s from a figure of 47 per cent of average earnings to only 18 per cent. It is furthermore the case that forms of supplementary benefit, to which many of the unemployed are entitled, are not taken up. In Britain such entitlements are claimed, apparently, in only 76 per cent of cases. According to the 'Households Below Average Income' survey in 1993 the average unemployed person's household income was £102 per week after housing costs. This was at the very bottom of the incomes pile and firmly in the lowest 20 per cent range of incomes, which is used as the benchmark for households in poverty.

In the coalfields it is easy to show that unemployment has aggravated all other forms of poverty. Low wages have become the rule in an area of intense competition for jobs; there are more lone parents as people have migrated in search of work; the long-term sick have notably increased in numbers; and many people have been prematurely retired.

The loss of income involved in the pit closure programme can be calculated without difficulty. The income from benefits, including sickness and other sources for an unemployed man, including housing costs, would not be more on average than £200 per week or just half what was earned on average by a working coal miner before. Such a halving of incomes is confirmed by the Statistical Office's Family Expenditure Surveys. These show households with an unemployed head of household spending only a little over a half of those with an employed head where both were manual employees. A particularly worrying aspect of the expenditure surveys is that expenditure on food is generally almost halved in households headed by an unemployed person.

The loss of income to the redundant miner is but a part of the loss to the local economy. Even though we saw earlier that only a quarter to a third of those losing jobs fell out of the labour force, another quarter left the area. Moreover, losses to the local economy would include reduced purchases by the collieries from local suppliers and the multiplier effect of reduced incomes. North Nottinghamshire Training and Enterprise Council estimated that the net income losses to the area from the 1992 pit closures involving over 8000 employees would total some £250 millions in miners' wages and £38 million in annual colliery spending, and this does not include the multiplier effect of lost incomes. The 1992 pit closures in North Derbyshire involved 6,500 men. The overall reduction of employment in the Notts and Derbyshire coalfield between 1982 and 1995 was some 45,000, more than three times the 1992 number. We can compare a financial loss of something of the order of £2,000 million from a total annual income from employment in the East Midlands as a whole of about £20,000 million in the early 1990s, i.e. a loss of 10 per cent.

Redundancies in the Derbyshire Coalfield

Such figures would be replicated throughout the coalfields. The loss of income was of course concentrated in a few villages and small towns where the effect was very much greater than a 10 per cent cut. All reports indicate that even those ex-miners who found work locally did so at much lower rates of pay. A Derbyshire County Council survey of

Redundant Mine Workers made in 1994 showed that just over half of the respondents had found work, but the average pay was £168 per week based on average rates of pay of £4 per hour; that was much less than half of the current underground mineworkers' rate. More than two-thirds of the partners of the respondents were working, nearly all of them part-time, a third of them for less than 16 hours a week. This would in no way make up for the man's loss of earnings, but might in some cases take the household income outside the level of eligibility for benefit.

Some questions might be raised about the representativeness of these respondents, since they constituted only a third of the 1800 mine workers made redundant from the three particular Derbyshire pits closed in 1993. What one can be sure of is that they will have comprised those who stayed in the area and of those the better educated ones, and the ones therefore most likely to have found work and to have got better pay. The least educated and least skilled will have found most difficulty in the labour market, but they are the least likely to have responded to the postal questionnaire. If anything the responses from the one-third are therefore likely to have given a more rather than a less rosy picture than the reality lying behind.

It is not surprising to learn that the coal miners made redundant and most likely to have found work were in the younger age range and included very few of the over 45s. Even amongst the young men who found work, it was in unskilled labouring, even when they had craftsmen's qualifications. The 1991 Census showed that in Derbyshire 26 per cent of the unemployed had been in craft or related work, but only 14 per cent of vacancies were from the appropriate productive side of the economy, according to a Derbyshire Welfare Rights Service report. This report also indicated that in half the job vacancies advertised the wage rates were lower than the Income Support threshold for single parents or couples with children.

It is interesting to note in the light of the Beatty-Fothergill study what had happened to the 252 men who were not working (46 per cent of the respondents in the Derbyshire survey):
* 23 were attending courses
* 40 were unable to work owing to ill-health or disability
* 40 had claimed unemployment benefit for 12 months and then due to their savings could not claim income support

* 3 had retired
* 146 – only just over a half of those not working – were actively seeking work while claiming benefit and would therefore be the only part of the non-working population of 252 included in the official count of the unemployed.

It is a striking fact about a period of high unemployment that households polarise into those with two earners and those with none. In this Derbyshire survey two-thirds of those who had found work had partners also earning with an average weekly combined income of £262. One in eight of the partners had started work only when the male head of the household became unemployed. At the other extreme, half of those not in work were in households where there was no other earner. Here the weekly income from benefit and support would be little over £100. Twenty-nine of these households had children under 16, in the meiotic words of the report, 'placing massive financial pressure on the households'. Eurostat figures for 1993 show the UK with the highest proportion of children of all Member-states in poor households (i.e. having less than 50 per cent of net average income). The proportion in coalfield areas must be even higher than the national figure of 32 per cent.

The response to redundancy in the Derbyshire study was almost universally negative, worse even than in the Shirebrook Skills Audit. No more than 30 men out of the 550 respondents saw positive results in a new and healthier life. A fifth felt depressed, demoralised, even devastated, and others added bitterness towards British Coal and the Government. Nearly half complained at having to accept a lower standard of living and having difficulty in finding employment. This was especially true for the over 40s. Even those in work did not regard their employment as secure. One half of those in work had already had at least one other job since redundancy as had a quarter of those out of work at the time of the survey. Many found their redundancy money was soon used up; and of course as time goes on this will be a larger and larger number. There was widespread complaint at the breakdown in networks and friendships, reduced social life and the closing down of local shops and clubs. Miners' welfare clubs had relied on a levy per tonne mined from British Coal to subsidise social, welfare and community activities in mining areas.

Redundancies in Yorkshire

There is nothing special about the Derbyshire Area. A two year research project, sponsored by the Economic and Social Research Council and the Rowntree Trust in 1993, into the problems faced by 500 miners made redundant in the Doncaster area of Yorkshire reached the following findings:

* many miners used their redundancy payments to pay off their mortgages on former pit and council houses. However, as the local economy could no longer offer jobs, they were left with an unsaleable asset, which restricted their ability to seek employment elsewhere;

* families who had invested their redundancy money did not qualify under social security rules which prohibit claiming benefit while having more than £8,000 in savings; (This would represent only £480 annual return, when invested at 6 per cent.)

* the few jobs which became available were paid considerably less than the amounts the miners were previously able to earn and often involved working longer hours;

* women often became the sole income earners but the level of pay was small in comparison with their partners' previous earnings;

* 75 per cent of redundant miners had been unable to obtain permanent employment two years after being made redundant;

* bitterness and despair ensued within families;

* loan sharks increased their business while the community 'traded down' to lower quality shops.

It has been the experience in all the coalfield areas that pit closures have led to an increase – ranging from 75 per cent to 100 per cent – in referrals to Social Services, demanding a doubling of local budgets. In a Derbyshire County Council 1992 study of *The Impact of Colliery Closures*, referrals are reported to have centred on:

* family poverty – demands on welfare rights, local budgets;

* family stress leading to breakdown and requests for children/young people to be accommodated with consequent demand to foster carers;

* individual stress related problems, e.g. depression/anxiety requiring intervention of mental health services; violence to women;

* increased demand for domiciliary services – unemployment and having more time available do not necessarily lead to increased care

for elderly relatives. In addition, families move away to find work leaving elderly people behind;
* more single parent families, as men emigrate to find work and after a time may not return because of housing and travel costs and new relationships; problems with maintenance payments.

The quality of poverty evidently cannot be conveyed only with statistics. We found one East Midlands school in 1994 where the head teacher realised that the children were not able to concentrate because they had not had any breakfast at home. He organised volunteers to put on breakfast in school before work started. Within a week or two he was approached by parents, who asked if they, too, could come to breakfast. Given the pride of most people in such a situation, their condition must indeed have been very pressing. The situation is often worst among households with a mortgage. We are back to the experience of Dr McGonigle on the Tyneside in the 1930s, who found the worst malnourishment on new housing estates where rents were higher than on the old.

Debt

An inevitable consequence of deprivation on this scale is the continuous growth of debt. The Mansfield Citizens' Advice Bureau tells us that more than 40 per cent of the enquiries it dealt with in 1996 were debt related. This problem came to the attention of the Mansfield and Bolsover District Councils, when they prepared their joint presentation to the Deputy Prime Minister, seeking to have the areas adjacent to the River Meden, within their two Districts, designated a 'transformation zone'.

The report of the North Nottinghamshire Training and Enterprise Council (September 1997) insists that financial stress is a serious problem, nonetheless acute because it has taken time to manifest itself. People exhaust their savings and their redundancy payments before they begin the abrupt descent into indebtedness. This descent is, however, unavoidable.

In the TEC Report we see that Ashfield and Mansfield are joint 413th in the ranking of 438 British districts for average disposable household income. This puts them amongst the very poorest districts, well down iin the lowest decile of household income distribution. Bassetlaw is at first sight in a happier position, since it figures at position

307 in the league table. But of course, Bassetlaw is a mixed district, with severe poverty concentrations in its coalfield areas, and large tracts of comfortable housing for the better-off, even the distinctly affluent, in other areas. The average may camouflage the general poverty, but it will not alleviate it.

The news that there are large concentrations of unemployed people, in a desperate financial situation, has attracted the loan sharks. A new directory, *The Unemployment Warehouse*, identifies areas in Britain with heavy concentrations of unemployment. Working from official statistics, the directory was originally intended to help mail order firms or credit companies to save money by avoiding advertising in those areas where most residents would be unlikely to be able to afford their products or services. Charities, too, were also able to save the costs of mail shots to people who were unable to afford to contribute to their causes.

But it was reported in the press that this directory was also being used for the opposite purpose from that for which it was originally intended. Armed with the directory, credit companies and loan sharks can actually target those who are without jobs, taking advantage of their desperate financial need. When people live in poverty for a long time, there is evidence that they can come to adjust to a life in debt. But for those who are precipitated from above average earnings into deep distress within a short period of time, debt can be a mortifying experience, contributing to the sense of hopelessness and rejection.

Unemployment and Ill-health

'Unemployment begets poverty, which begets ill-health and premature death.'

These were the words of the *British Medical Journal* in a famous editorial published at the beginning of August 1992. The *Journal* was considering the publication of a study of mortality and social organization, which concluded that unemployment was a direct cause of mortality among men seeking work.

At that time, 2.7 million Britons were out of work. Had the count been organized on the same basis as that used in 1979, the numbers would have been much higher: at least a million more. As things were, 2.7 million people represented 9.6 per cent of the total workforce. There are, of course, changes in the levels of unemployment, between regions, cities, and townships. New employment possibilities do materialize, and the jobs that they provide reduce the unemployment statistics within a catchment area which will depend to some extent on the efficiency of transportation systems, and to some extent on the availability of appropriate mixtures of skill in areas round and about the new installations. Jobs have been engendered in the coalfield, too. But the overall rates of employment have improved but slowly, and patchily, since 1992. Then, wrote the *BMJ*,

> 'Poverty and ill-health are so closely related ... in the most recent survey of occupational mortality, 62 of the 66 major causes of death among men were more common in unskilled and partly skilled men; 64 of the 70 major causes of death in women were more common in their wives. The poor pay for their poverty with their lives.'

Dr Richard Smith went on to report in the *BMJ* that the incidence of suicide among unemployed men runs at twice the level suffered in the general population, whilst the premature death rate is one-third higher.

In May 1993, no doubt influenced by these findings, the Trent Regional Health Authority commissioned a two year research project from the University of Nottingham, in order to assess the levels of health in the coalfields. Three Reports have so far been produced by the team engaged in this research. The first of these concerned the effect of unemployment on health in the area around Silverhill colliery, which closed in April 1993. The study was based in Sutton in Ashfield and Skegby. The second Report was called *The Three Mines Study*, and surveyed 3,161 people, including 1,064 miners who were working during 1992-3 at either Annesley Bentinck, Welbeck or Bilsthorpe collieries. The third study was a follow up survey, matching 780 people who had taken part in the earlier programme.

In the first, Silverhill, study, more than 400 people were surveyed, and useable responses were gathered from some 300. The survey found that unemployed men suffered more from psychological problems such as depression and boredom than did employed men. A smaller proportion of unemployed men had access to social support. Unsurprisingly, unemployed men suffered greater financial strain than did employed men. Their physical health was also worse than that of those who remained employed. Unemployed men apparently were likely to reduce their physical leisure activity, and to eat a less healthy diet. They were then more likely to visit their General Practitioner for consultations. The survey found that unemployment places a stress on families and relationships, and cuts back social contacts, undermining a number of social institutions such as the Miners' Welfare. But women with unemployed partners were found to be drinking more, and entering into more frequent binges, or periods of sustained drinking, than were women with working partners. The Social Audit of the Coalfield Communities' Campaign (1997) quotes the 1991 Census: it 'asked people whether they considered themselves to have a limiting long-term illness. Over three-quarters of a million people of working age living in the coalfield said they did.'

Unemployed Miners: Stress and Suicide

The second study, which included the working miners at the three collieries mentioned above, made possible even more detailed comparisons. 1,236 useable responses were gathered in this survey. It showed that both unemployed and working miners were disadvantaged in terms of psychological health, compared to working non-miners. 45.2 per cent of people who were either working or unemployed miners, or unemployed non-miners, were suffering psychological disorders, compared to 23.4 per cent of working non-miners. All the unemployed, as well as the current miners, were worse off in terms of psychological health: but they also were disadvantaged in terms of physical health and vitality.

Unemployed miners in particular were more likely to be teetotallers or excessive drinkers than were working miners. They were also likely to have less social support, and were less likely to have a current partner. It may not be thought surprising that they were also found to have lower levels of self-esteem. Over the year between the two studies, 52 per cent of the unemployed miners had gained weight, compared with 39.7 per cent of the working miners. Overall, 10.2 per cent of unemployed miners were actually obese, compared with 6.8 per cent of working miners. 41.8 per cent of unemployed miners were smoking every day, and unemployed miners were four times more likely to have increased their smoking than were the working miners. Just over half the unemployed miners were convinced that their level of physical activity had deteriorated. This was double the proportion of working miners reporting the same feeling. The financial stress experienced by unemployed miners also ran almost twice as high as the financial strains reported by working miners, even though the immediate impact of unemployment on miners had been cushioned by enhanced redundancy settlements.

The third study was able to show an improvement in psychological health among those who had remained in mining, and an even larger improvement in the psychological health of the unemployed miners who had found alternative employment. 22.4 per cent of those who had stayed inside the mining industry showed better psychological health, and almost 40 per cent of those who had been unemployed and then found alternative jobs were in better psychological trim. Formerly unemployed miners who had got alternative jobs were more likely to perceive improvements in the problem solving support available to them, if they had moved into their new jobs. But among those remaining unemployed, the levels of practical support were seen as declining. There was a further decline in the emotional support available to unemployed miners. 14.3 per cent of them reported deteriorations in their emotional environment, compared to half that proportion of miners still at work. 21.7 per cent of the unemployed miners had become binge drinkers, compared with only 8.1 per cent of the current miners.

The researchers concluded that there was a continuous need for counselling services to deal with these psychological stresses, and to help in practical problem solving.

The summation of these three studies was followed by an analysis of data gained from General Practice consultations. 798 responses in the 1995 survey could be matched to the earlier investigation of 1992. The result gave serious cause for concern. It showed that there was an increase of about half in the levels of stress about money. The proportion of people 'very satisfied' with their social life declined from 28.1 per cent to 19.3 per cent. People's self-assessments of their strength and stamina diminished perceptibly. Smoking was on the increase, and personal relationships were deteriorating. The percentage of women who had former miners as partners who reported that they 'had someone they felt close to' went down from 90.7 per cent to 80.1 per cent. Those women who were 'stressed out about work' increased from 23.3 per cent of the total to 30.5 per cent. Self-assessed stamina also declined, and drinking increased by an average of two units per week.

The researchers concluded that the lack of job opportunities compounded the problem of poor health.

'Unemployment whether official or unofficial, is normally associated with low income. It is concerns about low income that are behind the increase in stress levels in mining communities.'

This stress in turn contributes to the deterioration of relationships, and an increase in smoking. There are numerous reports of increases in drug taking in coalfield communities, which presumably follow a similar pattern.

'Unless action is taken this worsening in lifestyle suggests future health problems and ultimately a shortening of life expectancy.'

All this stress has been picked up by the caring Social Services, and the voluntary bodies working in these areas. The Samaritans, for instance, reported that their office in Worksop in the Nottinghamshire coalfield had experienced a significant increase in suicide calls over recent years, and told the *Worksop Guardian* (27.10.95): 'We want to open 24 hours a day. At the moment it is 8 hours. There is a definite need for it.' But the branch met current levels of need with a staff of 40. Many more volunteers would be needed if the phone were to be open all day through. Nearby in Mansfield, the local Samaritans reported that they had received 1,373 suicide calls in the twelve months before November 1995. 291 of these calls were classed as involving an active risk of suicide, and 81 of them came from people who were actually commiting suicide at the time. Of course, not all of these crises involved unemployed miners. But a growing number did.

The national trend has been towards a significant increase in the mortality of unemployed people as compared to others of working age, and a higher level of mortality among younger men. This trend has been confirmed in a number of areas. In Seaham for instance, on the North East coast of Britain, there used to be three coalmines employing more than 5,000 men. In November 1995 the *Sunday Times* reported that Canon Paul Jobson, vicar of St. John's, had said that: 'He has conducted the funerals of more suicide victims' since his arrival in the Parish six years ago, than in the whole of the previous twenty-five years of his Ministry in London and other areas of Britain.

'Eighteen suicides', he says solemnly. 'Twelve of them were ex-miners, two were teenagers without employment and the rest were women who could not cope. Many drank themselves to death. Others took their lives by more instant means – the deep waters of the sea, the rope and the overdose ... The Durham town has a suicide rate four times the national average, placing it among the highest in Britain.

'The last deaths were in July, when two people jumped from Seaham's North Pier. Jimmy Smith, 32, a former miner, was spotted at 5.30 one morning jumping into the sea ... Billy Smith, the brother of the dead man said: "Like many ex-miners, Jimmy was depressed and down because he had no prospect of finding work. He worked in the pits for nearly ten years. He is not alone. Many others feel exactly the same way."'

The difficulty involved in measuring suicide is that despair takes many forms, and has many ways of destroying people. The *Sunday Times* told us that in Seaham 'many drank themselves to death'. Anyone who did that in another town might very well not end up on the list of suicides. Many other people end their lives with an overdose. Is that a deliberate desire to leave the world, or has it been 'death by misadventure'? Whether it is registered as suicide or not, it is often death out of hopelessness, just as surely as desperation drove so many Seaham miners to jump into the sea, or to hang themselves.

This difficulty means that suicide statistics are especially open to dispute. But the official record tells it like this: since the early 1970s 'suicide rates among men have been rising, while rates for women have continued to fall'. *Social Trends*, published by the Central Statistical Office, can go deeper than this. Older men have been less prone to commit suicide, 'while the rates for men aged between 25 to 44 have risen to such an extent that they now exceed the rates for those aged 45 to 64'.

The Office of Population Censuses made enquiries. Their research shows that younger men who remain single, or encounter marital difficulties, or become divorced, may account for as much as half of the increase in suicides since the 1970s. 'Of course this age group of men has also been affected by other factors ... such as high unemployment rates'.

Crime and Drugs

The link between rising unemployment and growing crime has been very clearly documented by John Wells (see *The Right to Work*, edited by Ken Coates, 1995). The *Social Audit* of the Coalfield Communities' Campaign (1997) reports that coalfield reported crime is now above the national average, and that the gap is widening. In formerly close-knit communities, this is a moral defeat which really hurts: as the CCC report: 'the fear of crime represents a major deterioration in the quality of life'.

A sinister part of this problem accompanies the extension of a widespread drug culture, about which we need to know a great deal more.

CHAPTER SIX

The Scope and Limits
of Self-help

It would give a totally false impression of the situation in the British
Coalfields if a picture was painted only of gloom and despondency.
A whole range of new initiatives has emerged from the grassroots in
the coalfields. The first was the Coalfields Community Campaign
(CCC) founded in 1985 and based in Barnsley at the centre of the
Yorkshire coalfield, with the financial support of local government
Councils. Its aim has been to represent the needs and interests of the
people of the coalfields, as employment in mining has been steadily
reduced. The Campaign has carried out research in association with
local universities, agitated on behalf of all those affected by the pit
closures and made representations for financial aid from local, national
and European funding agencies. It is an active member of EURACOM
which represents over 450 mining communities in seven European
Union Member-states and it did much to obtain the special RECHAR
funding for coalfield regeneration from European Union funds. It has
also given support to local educational and training programmes, which
we will look at later.

The CCC is an umbrella body having official backing, but the spirit
of self-help can sometimes be more clearly seen at the village level. We
will take one example in Nottinghamshire, which has already attracted
international attention.

The Boughton Energy Village
An initiative in the East Midlands coalfield illustrates the richness of
grassroots efforts at self-help in the face of high unemployment resulting
from pit closures. A group of councillors in North Nottinghamshire
have taken up some highly imaginative proposals from the District

Architect. These are all designed to combat fuel poverty, cut back imported energy supplies, reduce heating costs and at the same time create employment. The scheme combines work on insulation of all present and one-time Council houses, new types of gas heaters and involves plans for a local power station fired by burning farm crop straw and coppiced willows. A central element in the scheme was the conversion of a disused arterial well pumping station, not only for demonstrating the use of bio-mass in power generation, but for an exhibition and training centre related to renewable energy and energy efficiency and for craft workshops and recreational facilities for local people and visitors. This project alone has attracted £2.5 million funding and will create 150 jobs and assist 25 businesses. Entitled 'Pumping Life back into the Coalfield Community', it won a Rural Development competition grant.

The long-term plans for 'Boughton Energy Village 2001', as it has come to be called, and the associated Sherwood Energy Village, go far beyond what has so far been achieved. It comprises nothing less than the conversion of the whole village to bio-mass driven electric power with enough energy to spare to provide for an artificial ski slope on the hill behind the village and a new tourist complex set around an artificial lake where the colliery once stood. We have seen the plans and we believe that, given initial funding, the enthusiasm of the local councillors and the District Architect could ensure their realisation. These will be unveiled at the first of a series of Energy and Environment Festivals to be held in Boughton during the year 2001.

In this respect, it is important to notice the reasons which are given in the Nottinghamshire Rural Development Area *Annual Review, 1995* for the success of the Boughton Pumping Station partnership project:

'Firstly, the extent of community participation which had taken place at an early stage and then sustained throughout the formative stages of project development.

Secondly, the strong commitment of the private sector to the project, most manifest in the involvement of Severn Trent Water as a key partner and the backing of the Ollerton and District Economic Forum.

Thirdly, the development of a strong local partnership comprising all the key players from the public sector including the Parish Council, the District Council, the County Council and the Training and Enterprise Council.

Finally, it is worth stressing that the proposals for Boughton Pumping

Station had been in gestation for a significant period of time, well before the time that the rural challenge was announced.'

How many more worthy and exciting project proposals rest in the filing cabinets of Coalfield Area District Offices, which could set hundreds of thousands of men and women to useful work, awaiting only the golden touch of initial funding to be activated?

Another significant example comes from Derbyshire, just across the county boundary from Mansfield. This is the Shirebrook and District Development Trust, whose skills audit we have already referred to. At the anniversary of the Trust's foundation in January 1995, just over a year after Shirebrook colliery was closed, the chairman gave the following report, published and printed in *Patchwork News*, the Trust's own local news sheet (to which we have added our own occasional comments in square brackets):

Shirebrook Development Trust

'Shirebrook and District Development Trust really began when a group of people with a range of skills and backgrounds [local councillors, local government officers, clergy, solicitors, headmaster, farmer, WEA tutor organiser, nurse, one-time NUM local branch officers] formed together to see what could be done through local projects. We knew that the only way forward was to stop looking for somewhere to point the finger of blame, to find ways of attracting new money to Shirebrook and to start singing the praises of the area's richest of natural resources, the skills and strong community spirit of the people.

Right from the beginning it was a gamble. The Trust convinced the Royal Bank of Scotland [one of the district councillors was a Scotsman!] to approve a loan allowing us to renovate some dilapidated local shop premises [in what had been the Old Main Street of the town, always referred to locally as 'Patchwork Row'].

The bank showed enough faith in what we were proposing to start things moving. We then approached other funding agencies for support and now less than a year on the Trust's list of achievements is, by any measure, considerable.

* The renovation of derelict property on Main Street. Shirebrook now provides home [not only to the Trust offices and printing room but] to the Derbyshire Unemployed Workers' Centre, the East Scarsdale [Church] Ministry, the Workers' Educational Association, and is soon to welcome Shirebrook Town Council [rates office], West Nottinghamshire College and new local businesses. [The renovation has since encouraged a pharmacy – opposite the medical practice – mortician, two women solicitors and the Job Centre to do up property and to locate in the same row.]

* A ground breaking Skills Audit [already referred to] involving thousands of local homes [almost a total house by house survey of Shirebrook, Creswell, Langwith and Whaley Thorns], conducted by and for local people, promises to overturn official figures on unemployment, skills, long term illness and social needs.
* Working with the Town Council to breathe new life into Shirebrook Town centre, is promoting the market and attracting new interest and new money to shops and businesses. We realised that the population of Shirebrook increases by 50 per cent on Market Day, making it our main attraction. With the help of Bolsover District Council, we increased free parking, tidied up the local area, developed new promotion material advertising Shirebrook – the Market Town. [This will be helped in 1998 by the reopening of the railway line – the Robin Hood Line – and railway station, as the result of strong Coalfield pressure and with the help of European Community funding].
* Initiating plans for a Town farm to be based at Shirebrook school and run in partnership with Derbyshire Agricultural College which will provide a base for rural studies plus educational and training opportunities within the next two years.

Shirebrook is not by nature a community of entrepreneurs, but has in the past been known for the hardworking traditional skills of its people. With the male unemployment in some wards [officially] topping 25 per cent and high long term illness levels as a legacy from the mining industry, we are battling against the odds, but we have no option, we either give up now or dig in and get on with it. Being out of work, as opposed to being in a secure job, makes you look at life differently. It attacks your morale and your confidence. We have to work together to regain the local community's confidence and use that to rebuild the future.

Bolsover District Council successfully secured funds from the Single Regeneration Budget and worked to forge links with Brussels and the wider European market from which Shirebrook will benefit. We have also had support from the Rural Development Commission, Derbyshire County Council, the area's Training and Enterprise Council, plus help from local businesses and individuals.

We have achieved a tremendous lot so far, but there is still a long way to go. I know the Trust has its fair share of critics. People who say – what's the point in doing up old shops and carrying out big research projects? But it's easy to sit back, do nothing and criticise.

The results of the work so far are there for all to see. A part of Shirebrook's town centre which was near-derelict a year ago, is beginning to welcome new paying tenants who are employing local people. [And there are new plans for renovating other buildings in the town centre with a historical interest.]

Information from the Skills Audit will provide us with the clearest picture yet of the range of skills held by Shirebrook people and their hopes for the future (and needs for education and training). Phase Two of the Audit will be using this information to develop a kind of CV for the town to which outside business agencies will be able to refer when considering whether to invest in the local area.'

On the basis of this audit there is little doubt that a major advance in education and community development can proceed. It is an impressive story, but it does not stand alone.

Self-help in the Environment

It would be quite impossible to do justice to the scope of community self-help initiatives in the coalfields without mentioning the enormous diversity of organisations which have come into being spontaneously to deal with environmental problems, many of which are a direct result of the working of coalfield industries. This comprehensive activity will be the subject of another book in the present series which will aim to draw lessons from a period of sustained campaigning, and to examine both its successes and failures.

Of course, the environmental consequences of the coal industry have been complex. Planners were easily persuaded that the industry created an unsightly mess. They have paid a great deal of attention to the resculpturing of pit tips, and the creation of new country parks where waste and spoil heaps were once omnipresent. The village of Grassmoor near Chesterfield, for instance, was dominated by its pit tip, which actually leaned against some of the houses. A visit to that old village, now long disappeared, was quite unforgettable. In the most distressing conditions, people did their best to live modern lives. But the old country values never died. A particularly poignant symbol of the old Grassmoor was the goldfinch, which lived in a cage, hanging from the front of one of the houses.

Millions of pounds have now been spent on the restyling of tips, and there are many former miners who wish that some of that money could have gone on investment in new jobs. But even the reshaped, landscaped environments which have been left behind have their own pollution problems. At Grassmoor, for instance, the lagoons which remain are contaminated with dioxins. Even the best intentions cannot easily cope with the squalid inheritance of the coal industry in parts of the coalfield.

There are four major ways in which local pressure groups have sought to recover a decent environment. First of all, there is the question of industrial pollution. Plants and chemical works which have been dependent on coal by-products have been associated with a history of dangerous contamination. In parts of North Eastern Derbyshire, dioxins have contaminated the rivers, soil and herbage. Local people have banded together in a number of associations, to monitor pollution, and to insist on cleaning up some of the most poisonous areas such as the site of the former Avenue Coking and Chemical Works at Wingerworth near Chesterfield, which is now owned by English Partnerships. Often campaign groups working on these problems feel strong pressure from vested interests, so that it takes some courage to maintain their activities. The famous presumption that 'the polluter must pay' is almost laughable in the face of the experience of coalfield people. The River Doe Lea, for instance, was briefly celebrated as 'the most poisonous river in Europe'. But it has never proved possible to find contributions from likely polluters to meet the costs of cleaning it up.

The closure of coal mines also contributes to another problem of contamination. By 1994 the National Rivers Authority had identified 200 kilometres of rivers, streams and brooks which had been contaminated by waters from abandoned coal mines. Legislative weakness has created the fear that this problem could be greatly aggravated during the coming years.

A second major matter for concern, which has given rise to village organisations and protesters over a wide arc of the coalfield region concerns opencasting and quarrying. The destruction of the deep mined coal industry was not complete, but it was very extensive indeed. Now those who operate the diminished industry insist that it is necessary to 'sweeten' deep mined coal by admixing coal from shallower seams, which is normally extracted by opencasting. There has been a prodigious extension of opencast mining, which makes more and more voracious demands on the coalfield countryside. Villages are encircled by these great cavities. Indeed, there have been pressing threats that whole townships could be surrounded by opencast workings.

The noise and dust generated in this work are obvious pollutants. But the dust is not simply unpleasant: it is a potent health hazard. When we began to monitor the extension of asthma in the coalfield area, we discovered some horrific concentrations in the vicinity of opencast workings.

With the change in Government it is possible that the rules governing planning applications could be changed, and that a long-standing demand of colliery villagers could be accepted, imposing a 'presumption against' opencasting, which would expect planning authorities to reject an application unless good cause could be shown to the local community that it could benefit them in some way. Up to now it has been almost impossible to prevent opencasting, if the contractor proposing it has been determined, and well endowed enough to pursue the expensive legal formalities. The threatened villagers have fought one case after another, usually with minimal resources. Their will to oppose has commonly been strong, however. Not only have they known in advance that the disruption of village life would be persistent and painful: they have also known that this method of extraction has become general only because of the extinction of one deep mine after another, and the imposition of misery on thousands of former miners.

A third concern of the environmental lobby unites it with people all over the country far outside the coalfields. It concerns the defence of wildlife habitats, public access to the countryside, and the quality of rural and urban life. It is worried about the widening of motorways, and involves a variety of campaigns for the reopening of amenities such as canals and waterways. Thousands of local people are involved in voluntary efforts to recuperate such amenities, whether in reopening the Chesterfield Canal from Worksop onwards, or in conserving the railway roundhouse at Barrow Hill in Staveley, or in dealing with the ill-effects of acid rain on historic buildings. Their experience of industrial pollution ensures that people in the coalfields are no less engaged to defend their heritage than the conservators of the Home Counties, or historic beauty spots.

And finally, the fourth matter of concern involves the disposal of waste, and tipping, and particularly the spread of toxic waste tips. Wherever an opencast void is created, there is a danger that someone will want to put something in it. Often that something will be very unpleasant. Sometimes it may be positively lethal. But there is much profit to be had from burying the detritus of our contaminant industries.

In every one of these four issues, there are dozens of activist pressure groups. Some have a long history, and others have mushroomed to deal with a crisis or threat. The activities of these people have been so intense that they have already given rise to a newsletter, *Direct Action*

News, which covers environmental action in the Derbyshire, South Yorkshire and Nottinghamshire coalfields. An extensive Green Festival has established itself in Worksop, as a meeting place for people who are engaged in this work.

Of course, the activity of friends of the environment alarms some industrialists, and makes their employees nervous. Higher standards, they feel, may result in further job losses, as pollutant behaviour becomes less acceptable. But the truth is that the effort to restore the coalfield environment is a major part of the effort to regenerate jobs and economic health. Areas of high atmospheric pollution are not areas which commend themselves to planners or investors, when they are seeking new locations for industry. The campaign to clean up is an evidence of the inextinguishable pride that coalfield people have in their neighbourhoods and communities. So many people and groups are engaged in this work that it would be invidious to single out one or another of them. But that is why it is necessary to examine and celebrate this resource in a different kind of book, designed to help in the work of recovery.

CHAPTER SEVEN

Education and Development Initiatives in the British Coalfields

oal miners had two advantages which could help in rebuilding
their shattered lives after the destruction of their industry. The
first was the traditional sense of community in the mining
villages, which was shown to be still very much alive during the last
miners' strikes, particularly in the organisations of miners' wives. We
have already taken note of this community sense. The second was the
tradition of self-education. You can still see the coal dust on the books
in the South Wales Miners' Union library in Swansea.

The long-term adult residential colleges – The Central Labour
College, Ruskin College, Coleg Harlech, Newbattle Abbey and
Northern College – each received their strongest initial support from
the mineworkers' unions. The unions in Nottinghamshire, Yorkshire
and Derbyshire, in Staffordshire and South Wales, all persuaded their
local universities to provide special day-release courses for them –
Nottingham and Wales between the Wars, with Sheffield, Leeds and
Keele in the 1960s and '70s. Before the final collapse of the industry, by
the early 1980s there were 100 Yorkshire miners on courses at Sheffield
and another 100 at Leeds, there were 60 from Derbyshire also on
courses at Sheffield, there were 100 from the Nottingham area at
Nottingham, and similar numbers at Keele and in South Wales. And the
courses the students were attending one day a week and in some cases
for two days lasted for up to three or four years and covered an
introduction to the whole field of economic, political and social studies.

Self-education among Coal Miners

There is no doubt that such self-education prepared many coal miners
for adapting to a change in occupation when the decline in their

industry accelerated. Unfortunately, we are talking about a very small proportion of the total numbers in the industry – a few thousand over the years compared with several hundred thousand employed in coal mining over those years. When unemployment grew in the early 1990s, the studies made by Leeds Metropolitan University in Yorkshire and Derbyshire revealed that only 8 per cent or 9 per cent took up some form of training or education. The coalfields were found to have very low levels of formal qualifications among those employed – in Yorkshire in 1993 a quarter with no formal qualification at all. A higher proportion than the national average had left school without any graded results, and this was especially true of men, despite the increase in craftsmen working in the coal industry. Among manual 'operatives', only 13 per cent of males and 10 per cent of females had attained NVQ level 3. When the unemployed were studied, levels of educational attainment were found to be even lower. In Yorkshire two-thirds of the long-term unemployed had no formal qualifications.

The numbers involved in self-education may have been small, but apart from the benefit for these few as the coal industry was cut back, there was a second result of the day release courses – of even greater importance when the industry was finally all but destroyed. This was that a significant number of those who had taken advantage of the union's educational opportunities had gone on to work not only as union officials but as tutors on the very courses they had started on and on similar courses set up by the WEA and by the TUC at local technical colleges and elsewhere. In the last wave of redundancies many miners seeking some educational preparation for obtaining new work have found that their tutors were ex-miners. The realisation that this was so has been a crucial reassurance in encouraging men to go back to school once more in their thirties and even in their forties and fifties.

In a labour force numbering hundreds of thousands of men forced out of their jobs over the quite short period of less than a decade, the fact of a few hundred miners a year leaving the industry with more education than they had at the school leaving age, would seem to have no more effect than a drop in the ocean. But their impact has been crucial to the educational work essential for the regeneration of the coalfield areas. It is an ex-day release course student who is sharing in the writing of this book, another led the team which made the Shirebrook Skills Audit, another still was involved in the Derbyshire

County Council study of redundant miners, and a whole group of ex-day release students enrolled at the Northern College in South Yorkshire have been developing the Coalfields Learning Project (CLP). In Durham and in South Wales also, ex-miners who had received their education as mature students were centrally involved in the crucial stages of what is called in the jargon of the time 'first stage capacity building' for community regeneration.

Community Education and Development

The East Durham Community Development Initiative, which was founded in 1993 to bring about social and cultural regeneration in a former coalfield area, was taken as one of the Case Studies in the European Commission Report, *Social and Economic Inclusion Through Regional Development,* prepared by a research team under the leadership of Professor Peter Lloyd and published in 1996. This initiative attracted the interest of the research team because of its success in drawing local people into morale building activity, setting up local community organizations where little or no pre-existing organizational structures existed. Sixteen development workers were placed at a number of sites to initiate community based development – through training schemes, environmental improvement, toddler groups, etc. The scheme was managed by a partnership of statutory bodies, local Councils and community representatives. Finance was obtained from RECHAR and a further bid for RECHAR II money had, according to the Lloyd Report, 'to be resubmitted due to perceived lack of 'economic' outputs – 'economic' here meaning directly creating jobs. This issue of social and economic aid has become a central one for the coalfields. Making men and women more 'employable' does not of itself create jobs for them to do.

The Coalfields Learning Project based on South Yorkshire was founded in 1994. It grew out of the outreach work in the local communities of the Northern College. It appears from its prospectus and plan to have successfully combined the social and the economic in its bid for funds. It has the aim of developing 'a structured approach to life-long learning in the UK coalfields'. It has support from Sheffield Hallam University, Barnsley and Doncaster TEC, RJB Mining, Yorkshire Water and the Councils of Barnsley, Doncaster, Rotherham, Leeds, Wakefield and Derbyshire County. The project received

RECHAR funding and has made a bid for RECHAR II funding in the light of the work already achieved.

In setting out the aims of the Coalfield Learning Project, the authors, all ex-miners working now at the Northern College, write:

'The culture of mining communities has been built up over many years. It has been inherited and transferred as miners have moved from areas where pits have been worked out to staff new mines, which opened at the beginning of the century, such as those in the Yorkshire and Derbyshire coalfields. Mining culture has many positive and transferable aspects, such as hard work for a fair reward, belief in the importance of social and economic justice, family and community values, comradeship and team working.

The decline of the industry has, however, revealed a number of negative aspects also:

* reluctance to accept retraining and education;
* belief in the inevitability of failure outside mining employment;
* insistence on retaining gender stereotypical roles;
* reluctance to train for work in 'non-macho' occupations.

In these circumstances, conventional approaches to training, and the type of provision offered, have met with only limited success, because they have failed to recognise the difficulties involved in the culture change facing former mine workers, some of whom neither recognise the value of education and training nor the need to match this to modern employer requirements. Furthermore, current training tends to offer the prospect of poorly paid, insecure jobs to men used to relatively high wages, thus constituting an additional disincentive.

The principle aim of the Coalfields Learning Project is to dismantle these barriers and provide a framework which enables former mine workers and their families to gain access to a broad range of educational and training opportunities, thereby increasing their employment prospects ... and to contribute to the creation of a culture of lifelong learning in the coalfields.'

It seems an ambitious objective, in which there is certainly a combination of the economic and the social, and the combination seems to have made possible a successful launching for the scheme. Continuing it will require new funds.

Education lies at the centre of the South Yorkshire project, rather than direct employment creation. In this respect it differs from the proposals in the Lloyd Report. And yet, in the Lloyd Report's emphasis on Community Economic Development, certain preconditions in a pre-planning process were proposed for such development which were almost exactly prefigured in the South Yorkshire project:

* initial implementation teams (Local Authority or independent professional) to service local partnerships, to assess community priorities, develop strategies and assist with initial management;
* local partnerships to ensure that all can make their contribution;
* local community based organisations and businesses brought into contact to work out an agenda for local development and employment creation;
* advice and guidance to community based organisations on the use and application of European Structural (and other) Funds and on project design and management;
* support for local area or neighbourhood regeneration agencies, which can take on the role of capacity building into the future;
* support for the activities of animateurs (independent professionals, seconded local officers, trained community residents) to facilitate local activities in job prospecting, community enterprise and promotion of active citizenship;
* resource centres to provide a focus for activity and nodes for information exchange and networking with government and employment agencies and employers.

A Network of Coalfields Learning Projects

The authors of the South Yorkshire project have seen one of their tasks as extending the network of learning projects further afield. Contacts with other areas made by the Coalfields Learning Project, specifically in Nottingham, Durham and South Wales, led to the formation in November of 1996 of a country-wide Partnership of Coalfield Adult Education, Training and Development Initiatives. Its aims are to promote exchanges of information about regeneration projects among former Coalfields communities both inside the UK and throughout Europe, to represent the educational needs of these communities, facilitate joint fund raising, publicise work done and promote and undertake appropriate research.

The emphasis in the South Yorkshire project is to be understood as being not simply on training for employment but on life-long learning for work and leisure including local community activity. The mix here of the economic and the social is based on a clear recognition that many of the unemployed can never hope to get another full-time job, but with a job share or part-time job they will have time for useful and enjoyable leisure activity. This will include community work, but for all of this they will need some education and training. Regeneration thus means something more than more jobs and the project must be judged by wider criteria than the cost per job.

It is pioneering work that has been done by the Coalfields Learning Project in developing a network of tutors, trainers and development workers connecting different organisations and different levels of involvement, all with close links to the expressed needs of ex-miners and their families. A small partnership Development Group has been formed among education providers and community development workers in Barnsley drawn from the public and voluntary sectors, to devise and initiate schemes and programmes for training the trainers. A trial course of two and a half days was put together and delivered by facilitators from the Local Training Board at the Ilkley Training Centre of Bradford City Council. The aim was to develop facilitation skills, team building, shared vision and a common model among the several different and disparate organisations involved.

An outstanding example of the project's work at the grassroots level has been with a Community Association around the now defunct Grimethorpe Colliery which gave to the world the internationally famous Grimethorpe Brass Band. The Association began its life as a neighbourhood watch scheme, which saw the need to address the causes of crime with particular relation to young people and their feeling of social exclusion. Contact between the Coalfield Learning Project tutor (an ex-miner himself) and the Association led to the identification of an appropriate programme of learning and to the involvement of other local voluntary organisations and the local College of Arts and Technology.

The course of study ran in the evenings over a 14 week period, with a three day residential period of study at the Northern College. The study programme designed to meet the needs of a leading group from the Association covered an introduction to the following subjects:
* Group management skills
* Team building
* Conflict management
* Business planning
* Money management
* Company and charity law

* Housing law and leases
* Fund raising
* Recruitment and retention of members.

Six of the group who completed all the elements in the course received credits through the South Yorkshire Open College. Some have gone on to further courses in Information Technology and in problems of Oppressive Discrimination and Equal Opportunities. Others have enrolled on follow-up Core Skills courses. Family learning courses have been added to the courses for groups and individuals.

The Grimethorpe Association has grown to 100 members and the groups involved in the project are addressing wider issues around social exclusion. A Report dated October 1996 from the CLP Development Tutor ends as follows:

> 'The incidence of crime has been reduced and contrary to recent depressing press reports, there is a renewed and growing community spirit across Grimethorpe.'

On the basis of the Grimethorpe experience, the CLP established development tutors for Barnsley, Doncaster and Rotherham, with Leeds and Wakefield to follow suit. Over a three year period the number of students the project is expected to recruit rises from 145 in 1995 to 1100 by 1998. Of these it is projected that by 1998, 600 will progress on to further education, 75 on to higher education programmes, 300 on to other training courses and 125 into employment. It is not a large number in relation to the 75,000 registered unemployed in South Yorkshire alone in 1994, two-fifths of whom had been out of work for more than a year. And, as we have seen, you could double those figures to include all those who would like work if there were any to be had. With more funds, far more schemes could be launched. There is no shortage of potential development tutors and as schemes evolve they generate their own tutors and developers.

North Nottinghamshire Training and Enterprise Council (TEC)

North Nottinghamshire is a predominantly rural area, which had a particularly large concentration of employment in the coal industry, spread out through a number of villages and small towns. In the 1980s the number of pits was reduced from 29 to 13 and by the 1992 closures seven of the area's 12 remaining pits were closed, with a loss of over

8,000 of the remaining 10,000 mining jobs. The direct loss of earnings was estimated at £150 million, with another £60 million losses from the indirect effects on another 7,000 jobs. Comparison with other areas affected by pit closures suggests that the North Notts economy experienced in the words of the Report by the Training and Enterprise Council 'a much sharper initial impact than other areas'. Economic activity rates, already low at 78 per cent in 1992, fell by the end of 1994 to 74 per cent and had not recovered in the next two years.

The North Notts TEC proposed three Coal Plans to meet the staged pit closures. For these the TEC received £12.74 millions, to promote investment, enterprise and growth, investment in the community and access to employment through education and training. In summarising the 'scale of achievement' in its *Final Coal Plan Evaluation*, the TEC claims the preservation or creation of some three thousand jobs in 1993-97 directly from TEC projects and what they more tentatively call 'the likely placement of some 6,200 people into work' over that period. If this can be upheld, it is a commendable record. The Report does not, however, seek to conceal the problems that remain, where the claimant unemployment rate is only just above the national average, but there is a particular problem of unemployment amongst the over 40s and in the words of the Report

'there is clear evidence from a number of sources, that average income levels are low and some evidence that financial hardship and personal debt problems may be increasing'.

As we have seen, that is something of an understatement, as the report itself quite clearly establishes elsewhere.

Equally worrying, along with low incomes despite improved employment numbers and despite the TEC's concentration on youth training projects, is the conclusion of the Report that

'levels of educational attainment remain low, relative to national norms ... with a deterioration in unauthorised absence and fewer students achieving at least one GCSE' and that 'participation in further education remains below national and regional levels'.

The Coal Plan training which was provided is accepted in the Report as being 'short term in nature and often customised to the immediate needs of the employer'. The Report makes important recommendations about widening the TEC's Open Learning Centres and 'Gateways Shops' so that the concepts of 'life-time learning in a learning community' can be realised. Of course, it will be necessary for young people and adults alike to have the flexibility and range of skills that new types of employment demand. But the final conclusion of the Report must stand that

> 'there is a case for giving more attention to the need for modernising the local economic base'.

And that implies investment of something more than £13 million to make up losses of annual earnings of the order of £200 millions.

Urban Education and Development

Much of this discussion has concerned the problem of unemployment in the pit villages. But of course there were urban collieries as well as those scattered across the countryside. Some older pits had actually been sunk within the confines of city boundaries. (Radford, Wollaton, and Clifton in Nottingham, for instance. These came to the end of their useful life in the late sixties.) In those far off days their workers, if they wished, secured transfers to other mines nearby, but outside actual city boundaries. Many Clifton miners, for instance, were offered transfers to the developing colliery at Cotgrave. But many others took advantage of the pit closure to accept their redundancy pay and transfer to other employment in the city. That was easy during a time of relatively full employment: but it became more and more difficult for those involved in later closures, as manufacturing industry found itself in a fierce squeeze during the stringent economic policies pursued by Mrs Thatcher's administration in the early eighties.

What were the community resources of miners living in the larger towns and cities? Of course, they would commonly share the same kind of extended family networks which sustained other workers, in different occupations, living next door, or in the next street. But as pit closures finished off the inner city collieries, more and more mineworkers were bussed out or drove out, often to newer collieries in the surrounding countryside, where their workmates would normally be drawn from a very wide catchment.

The fond recollections of close-knit village communities remained true in certain areas, right up to the 1980s. During the great miners' strike, this sense of community became a physical presence, and withstood the most terrible hardships.

But the dispersion of urban miners into rural collieries was the least of the factors weakening old community ties. Whole coalfields were resettled in growing parts of the mining industry, during the decades of rationalisation and development before the eighties. In those days one of the most touching sights at the miners' galas was that of the grandparents getting back on the buses to take them home to the North, after having made the trek to meet their grandchildren during the fete and gala. Tearful reunions and tearful partings made manifest the pain of separation which had torn these communities apart when the able-bodied young migrated two hundred or so miles into nice new colliery housing with none of the social support networks that had grown up in the older traditional villages.

For the women in particular, these colliery villages were far from idyllic. Isolated from the shops, and from any possibility of female employment, they were ill-served by amenities of any kind. When unemployment struck the miners, it fell with redoubled force on these particular victims.

But in town and country alike large numbers of these workers remained unemployed and isolated, at a time when employment was everywhere hard to find.

It was like that in Nottinghamshire; the Local Education Authority, the County Council, had needed to take action to deal with the sudden surge in unemployment when the mines closure programme was speeded up after 1990. Education and training seemed to be the most urgent need and a programme called 'Fast Forward' was launched by the Council. The aim was to provide access to education at appropriate levels starting with basic literacy and numeracy and progressing onwards with both professional and volunteer tutors from the communities. Within two years nearly two thousand unemployed workers in the ward with the highest unemployment had been helped to go through the programme. The help comprised not only the provision of tutors and accommodation, but support towards travel costs, child care costs and some individual support for materials and fees. The Council itself obtained grants from various Government Challenge schemes.

Then it was the turn of the village collieries in Nottinghamshire which had been closed. The Council decided to apply the lessons learned from the urban 'Fast Forward' programme to the countryside. The central lesson was the need to break the barriers to access by placing the schemes firmly within local communities, in terms of both venue and organisation and quite distinct at first from the regular educational programmes. Support had to be made available for transport, child care and other costs. Progression could then be opened up into further courses with development tutors to advise on the different pathways.

One example of the community link was the establishment under the 'Fast Forward' programme of a centre staffed by a guidance adviser from West Notts College in the Shirebrook Development Trust complex described earlier. Funds are being sought under the RECHAR scheme for opening up an Education Centre in the middle of Shirebrook to provide a home for a whole range of educational and training activities. Already, the Trust runs jointly with the WEA a 'Media and Publishing Training Centre' with a dozen personal computers, printers and desk-top publishing equipment and access to 'E' Mail and the Internet. Eight courses are running each week with a total enrolment of about 50. For the unemployed any of these courses is completely free; for others the charge is £1 per hour.

There is a similar centre, the Community Learning Opportunities Centre (CLOC), in nearby Whaley Thorns, a village with the highest and longest record of unemployment in the area. This is owned by North Derbyshire Tertiary College and results from vigorous and enthusiastic pressure by the local councillor, Eileen Goucher, and her husband, a former miners' day release student. The Shirebrook Skills Audit, which included Whaley Thorns, revealed only 136 men and women with diplomas or degrees out of the 3600 who completed questionnaires, but 388 men and 366 women had some vocational qualification (GNVQ, RSA, City & Guilds, HNC, OND, HND, OND) and 419 men and women had computing skills. Many of them were not in work. Whaley Thorns may never be a 'Silicon Valley", but there are skills there which with a little further training should be attractive to outside investors and valuable for developing future trainers. And so it appears to be from the evidence of other Coalfield educational and training schemes.

A further several thousand in Nottinghamshire and Derbyshire can thus be added to the Yorkshire total of coalfield unemployed who have been restarting education, and similar schemes are being developed in Durham, Wales and Scotland. Supposing, rather optimistically at the present rate, that these schemes come to reach a total of 20,000 students up to the end of the century, that is still no more than one-tenth of those made unemployed by the closure of the mines and one-twentieth of the 1995 figure of registered unemployed men and women in the coalfield areas. Taking the hidden unemployed into account the educational provision currently funded will be serving no more than two to three per cent of those affected. These figures are not much to be proud of and still leave an aching void to be filled.

The value of this educational provision should not, however, be underestimated. A Sheffield University survey conducted in 1994 of coalminers in Yorkshire and Derbyshire who had attended the University's three-year courses on a paid day release basis at the Extra-mural Department revealed a considerable advantage for those who had attended the courses. Although 90 per cent of the respondents had left the industry and half of these were still out of work, including 15 per cent retired from old age or sickness, it was found on the positive side that 10 per cent were on further training schemes and most of those in jobs had used further education to advance their situation. Half were in white collar jobs and with better pay, and naturally regarded education as the key to re-employment. The most striking distinction among respondents was not so much that between the employed and the unemployed, as that between households without children where both partners were employed and households with children and only one partner or none employed.

The recommendations from the survey emphasised the importance of providing all necessary financial supports – extra benefit, no fees, child care, reimbursement of travel expenses, help with learning materials, etc. – for those undertaking education and training at all levels including higher education. The contrasting position of those who had not attended such courses as those at Sheffield University was not examined in the report. Their overwhelming number, however, must imply that, while education and training may be a necessary condition for re-employment they are not a sufficient condition. That requires positive measures by government to create new employment opportunities.

CHAPTER EIGHT

Sources of Funding for Coalfield Regeneration

Funds have been sought from a very wide range of sources for helping the large numbers of unemployed men and women in the Coalfield areas. Often the sponsors of a scheme, like the Northern College or the Shirebrook Development Trust, or even the Training and Enterprise Councils and Nottinghamshire County Council's 'Fast Forward' scheme are themselves dependent on funding from central government, directly or indirectly. Frequently such intervention involves controls by government bodies. This is true in the UK nowadays for the bulk of Local Authority expenditure; only about 15 per cent being now raised by the local Council Tax.

UK Sources

Special funds of two main kinds have been available for the Coalfield Areas. The first was the much heralded £1 billion package in 1992 (DTI Press Notice, October 13th, 1992) for 'redundancy payments and measures to help the communities affected', as promised by Michael Heseltine, when he was at the Department of Trade and Industry. This was designed to buy off the widespread protests following the announcement of the accelerated pit closure programme. But what happened to it? Apart from the money for redundancy payments, a sum of £200 million was mentioned by Mr Heseltine in March of 1993 to be enhanced by European Community funds. A sum of £75 million was provided to Training and Enterprise Councils, £30 million for 1992/3 and £45 million for 1993/4. A programme of property and sites provision was agreed with English Estates, later renamed English Partnerships. Details of expenditure under a partnership with the Urban Regeneration Agency are not available, but do not appear to have been very large, although it is rumoured that considerable sums are still undisbursed. There was some extra funding for new Enterprise Zones to be introduced 'where they would be most effective'.

A Coalfield Areas Fund was established with the risible sum of £5 million over two years for Local Authorities' activities in raising skill levels and encouraging new investment. Finally British Coal Enterprise and the Rural Development Commission were empowered to operate a scheme for retraining redundant miners with loans for job creation of £5,000 per job for a five year period at below the market rate for borrowing. (The usually accepted figure is nearer £9,000 per job, which would only provide 450 jobs out of the £5 million.)

These figures are all taken from Derbyshire County Council's *Impact Study of Colliery Closures*, dated October 1992. It is quite incredible that such a scheme could be considered acceptable as any sort of compensation for the loss of what was said to be 30,000 jobs but turned out to be a loss of nearly 40,000. At that time the Miners' Union refused to talk about such economic compensation but only about retaining pits in production.

British Coal Enterprise

British Coal Enterprise was established by British Coal in 1984, in anticipation of the need to redeploy coal miners and encourage the relocation of industry in coalfield areas. Its work covered three distinct fields. It was empowered to offer loans and equity finance to new and small businesses. It could provide work space in coalfield areas, some of which was purpose built, and it offered help in the placement and training of former British Coal employees who had been made redundant.

By 1996, the organisation claimed to have 'helped nearly 131,000 people into new jobs in under twelve years'. BCE staff were reported to have guided more than 60,000 redundant British Coal employees into new jobs. They were said to have created nearly 55,000 new jobs, not all of which went to former employees of British Coal, as a direct result of their business funding arm, which made loan and equity investments in coalfield businesses. And 16,000 job opportunities were created in the industrial units which were built or converted in mining villages and towns. The company's final report also claimed to have 'created 27,916 job opportunities' in the Midlands area.

But the Coalfield Communities Campaign had previously subjected this track record to some agnostic scrutiny. BCE's figures were, they said, 'seriously misleading'. The language used in BCE reports was calculated to accentuate the positive. Invariably they spoke of jobs 'assisted', not of jobs 'created'. Their talk was all of 'employment opportunities', not 'jobs'. This kind of reassuring vocabulary has subsequently been used by others. But it cannot be accepted without risk. As the Coalfield Communities Campaign itself insisted (*An Evaluation of British Coal Enterprise*, Stephen Fothergill and Nigel Guy, September 1994)

> 'The correct measure of effectiveness is **the number of jobs that would not have existed in the coalfields in the absence of BCE**, which is not what BCE's figures measure.'

Fothergill and Guy estimated that up to March 1994 BCE had created approximately 16,000 jobs in the coalfields, 'of which 2,000 were still-in-the-pipeline rather than on-the-ground'. About two-thirds of the new jobs were attributable to financial support for small businesses. Many of these new jobs did not go to former employees of British Coal, although they did provide work in the coalfield areas.

But in terms of the expense involved, the CCC saw this effort as 'a creditable performance'. BCE's support for business, and its provision of work spaces cost an average of between four and six thousand pounds per job. The placement services were more expensive, but they compared favourably in cost with other Government funded initiatives. But between 1984 and 1994 British Coal had shed almost 230,000 jobs, so that BCE could be argued to have made good 'just one in fourteen of the losses'.

Of course, British Coal Enterprise found itself working alongside Local Authorities, who responded in different ways to its efforts. Some were very satisfied, but others were quite critical. The placement service was generally rated highly, but the provision of work space was unevenly distributed, and there was naturally some criticism from Authorities which regarded themselves as having been left out. The Coalfield Communities Campaign surveyed the view of the Local Authorities in its membership, and reported on BCE's contribution to the regeneration of the coalfields. Based on Local Authorities' responses, they were able to calculate the impact of BCE on job creation, comparing one region with another.

Table 8
The Impact of BCE on Job Creation by Region, March 1984-March 1994

	British Coal job loss	BCE estimates of jobs 'assisted'	CCC estimates of jobs actually created in coalfields
Scotland	12,200	11,322	2,100
North	23,600	13,187	2,200
Yorkshire	47,300	21,875	3,100
Midlands	47,100	20,189	2,600
Western	17,400	18,188	3,000
South Wales	20,000	15,490	2,600
Kent	2,800	1,367	200
Not allocated by region	57,600*	4,411	300
Total	228,000	106,029	16,000

Regions are BCE areas.
*White collar and other staff. Regional figures are men on colliery books.
Source: *An Evaluation of British Coal Enterprise* by Stephen Fothergill and Nigel Guy, Coalfield Communities Campaign, September 1994.

Table 8 shows that between March 1984 and March 1994 there had been job losses in British Coal of 228,000, and BCE claimed to have assisted 106,029 people. But the jobs actually created in the coalfields numbered 16,000, or between one in ten in the North, and one in twenty in the Midlands Region or Yorkshire, in each of which more than 47,000 people had been displaced from work.

There has been a genuine statistical problem in identifying the responsibility for job creation. The CCC reported:

'BCE plays a helpful role, but given its staffing and resourcing it has never been more than a marginal player in the regeneration game. Indeed, it is worth bearing in mind that many of the projects assisted by BCE will also have received assistance from several other agencies – perhaps Local Authorities or English Estates with premises, central Government with grants, and TECs with training. Even if the jobs are genuinely new and additional, all the agencies involved could and probably do legitimately claim some credit.'

Nonetheless, BCE did make a contribution, and it was much valued in the coalfield areas. But in 1996, British Coal Enterprise came to an end. Privatisation split the organisation's three business divisions into separate companies. The funding division, which provided loans to businesses, was sold to a management buy-out team. The workspace company was taken over by a property group known as Birkby. This is a public limited company with an issued share capital of £49 million. And the job placement and career guidance section, Grosvenor Career Services, was also the subject of a management buy-out.

An estimated twenty-five per cent of the existing staff were made redundant straight away. They came from the organisation's head office in Nottingham.

On the 15th October 1996, the MP for Sherwood, Paddy Tipping, asked the President of the Board of Trade what sum was received by the Government from the sale of British Coal Enterprise. At that time, the response was that the sale was a matter for British Coal. 'I understand', said Mr Richard Page, 'that the Corporation has not yet completed the sale of all the activities of BCE'.

In fact, the Enterprise business funding arm of BCE was sold to the management buy-out team, and completion was announced in a press release dated 10th April. The new company, Coalfield Investments, had financial backing from the BancBoston Capital Limited, part of the Bank of Boston.

The other management buy-out, involving Grosvenor Career Services, was announced on the 26th April. The new company was backed by Granville Private Equity Managers with banking facilities provided by the Bank of Scotland. It was based in Derby.

Negotiations for the takeover of the workspace arm of British Coal Enterprise appear to have been more difficult. It was not concluded until January 1997. The present owners are Imex Enterprise Limited, a subsidiary company of Birkby PLC. This conducts the management of the workshops, from the regional centres. The Midlands Regional Manager informed us that he would like to expand the amount of workshop space held in the coalfield 'if it is commercially viable'. Since the privatisation they have doubled the occupancy of the Ollerton workshops. But this appears simply to mean that they have succeeded in letting workshops which they had taken over while they were empty. Imex Enterprise is discussing with various District Councils about further possible projects.

The Chairman of Birkby opened his Annual Statement on 30th June 1997, by saying:

'The most significant event for Birkby in the year ended 31st March 1997 was the successful acquisition of British Coal Enterprise Ltd (BCE). In one move, Birkby almost doubled the number of workspace centres managed by the Group, underlining our position as the UK's leading provider of managed commercial property to small and medium sized businesses.'

The Chief Executive reveals that these assets were acquired at a bargain price. In his Report he tells shareholders that the company paid £16.7 million for assets valued at £24 million at the date of acquisition, and that it is now worth £26.4 million.

The two management buy-outs rested on a great deal of existing experience of the coalfield, and of the needs of the coalfield communities. But privatisation not only loosened the constraints of subordination to the needs engendered by contraction in the coal industry: it also shifted the pattern of opportunities which would determine the future development of the newly independent enterprises. Business funding is a wider remit than coalfield recovery, and it leads to areas very far removed from the old mines. Out-placement similarly offers a wide range of contracts. Most recently, Grosvenor Career Services has been working to find placements for NAAFI staffs, and David Pickering, the Director, freely admits that the company goes after private contracts 'wherever possible'. Recently, his team have been working for the privatised railway sector and for National Power, for instance.

There has also been a quiet shift of emphasis by Coal Investments. They 'prefer to operate with established companies with better security and less risk'. They have stopped providing loans for less than £25,000, or offering start-up funding. The 'fast track' loans, which were unsecured, have also gone under. But these facilities were of major significance to would-be entrepreneurs among the redundant miners. The ease of access to credit was also a star point of the old BCE. They could lend where a bank or commercial lender would judge the risks insupportable. Once a small businessman has mortgaged his house, he has normally run to the limit of his potential credit. But BCE could take him beyond that limit, if the enterprise seemed viable and likely to promote employment.

Although Coal Investments have put up £1.5 million in loans since the privatisation, they have apparently withdrawn completely from this kind of socially justified lending. The complaints of Nottinghamshire County Council have thus turned out to be justified. Before the privatisation, BCE had been a funding partner in more than half of the County Council's financial assistance packages. Other sponsors have come forward, but it is safe to say that the conditions for financial support will not have been so closely tailored to the needs of redundant miners.

English Partnerships

English Partnerships was formed from a number of agencies, following the enactment of legislation on housing and urban development in 1993. In November that year, it took over City Grant, and it became fully operational at the beginning of April 1994, when it took over Derelict Land Grant and English Estates.

The Agency is charged with the task of encouraging the regeneration of areas of need through the reclamation, development or redevelopment of land and buildings. It is charged, wherever possible, to work with local and regional partners, in order to facilitate an all round approach to the tackling of the problems which come into its orbit.

> 'Its programme will address the need for land for a variety of purposes, including housing, industrial and commercial premises, the attraction of inward investment, infrastructure, leisure, recreation and environmental improvements'.

In 1996 English Partnerships accepted the transfer of approximately 5,600 acres of 'the most difficult and contaminated' sites from British Coal. These were part of an enormous portfolio, including 150,000 acres of agricultural land, commercial sites and residential property, as well as the darker inheritance of colliery waste tips and coking works. British Coal were supposed to have disposed of this entire portfolio before the end of 1996. Where they could, they gave the tips to Local Authorities, and tried to sell off the more desirable assets.

The poisoned chalice which came to English Partnerships consisted of 56 sites. A business plan was elaborated to deal with these, and it involved an investment of some £300 million over 10 years, in order to reclaim 2,125 acres for recreational and forestry purposes. The business plan estimates that up to 52,500 new jobs will be created as a result.

Parts of the portfolio could be exploited without such intensive preparations, and by Autumn 1997, there were already construction contracts on 20 per cent of the portfolio.

This work involved the search for useful partners, and high on the list of these was the Coalfield Communities Campaign.

In October 1997, English Partnerships was among the active bodies involved when Deputy Prime Minister John Prescott announced the establishment of a Task Force 'to put new life back into coalfield communities'. This was charged to identify the extent to which 'existing Government programmes might better support the regeneration of coalfield areas; the scope for best possible co-ordination and implementation of regeneration efforts across different departments and agencies; how partners such as Local Authorities, TECS, development agencies and the private sector might complement each other more effectively; and the ways in which the external funding for coalfield regeneration, for example, from the European Union, the National Lottery and the private sector, could make the best use of funding available'.

The Managing Director of English Partnerships, Paula Hay-Plumb, was appointed to chair the Task Force, which includes representatives from Government Departments, the Coalfield Communities Campaign, and other public bodies involved in working to regenerate coalfield areas.

During the seminar which launched this Task Force, almost all of the participants spoke of the need for substantial increases in the funding available for the work in hand. But no announcement was made about the provision of any additional funds.

European Sources

European Structural Funds are channelled through the national government and normally must be supported by matching funds from central or local government or from elsewhere. This requirement of what is called 'additionality' has seriously restricted the actual availability of European funds, especially where poorer Local Authorities in Britain like North-East Derbyshire have no longer been able to draw upon national resources for redistribution between rich and poor areas.

There are several different funds:

* European Regional Development Fund (ERDF) to promote 'balanced economic development throughout the Community';

* European Social Fund (ESF) to improve employment opportunities, especially through vocational training;
* European Agricultural Guidance and Guarantee Fund (EAGF);
* Specialised Community Initiatives for areas which are heavily dependent on one declining industry: RECHAR for coal, RESIDER for steel, RENAVAL for shipbuilding, RETEX for textiles, KONVER for defence;
* Research and Development Funds – for example, ESPRIT for information technology; THERMIE for energy technology innovation; LIFE for environmental protection; BRITE/EURAM for science and technology in manufacturing; DRIVE for improved transport services.

For applications for the first three funds, the European Commission has in the past determined five priority categories and it is clear that some of the coalfields could qualify under one or more of the five objectives (with qualifications indicated).

Objective 1, to narrow the gap between the least favoured regions and other parts of the Community. (Limited to areas where the per capita GDP is less than 75 per cent of the EU average. British coalfields have not, so far, been recognised as falling below the levels applying in such regions.)

Objective 2, to revitalise regions affected by serious industrial decline. (The coalfields have one of the strongest claims under this objective.)

Objective 3, to combat long-term unemployment and to integrate young people into the job markets. (The coalfields have an equal claim with other blighted areas under this objective.)

Objective 4, is to facilitate the adaptation of workers to industrial change and to change in product systems. (Possibly applicable to coal miners.)

Objective 5a, to adjust agricultural structures and

5b, to develop rural areas. (Pit villages have no special claim here.)

Objective 6, for Finland and Sweden.

The European Commission has always insisted on respect for three basic principles (but these have not always worked, as the comments in brackets below indicate):

1. Partnership. Active involvement of all who can contribute at all levels (but co-ordination in any district or region may prove difficult);

Table 9
EU Regional Aid to British Industrial Areas 1994-99

	£ million, 1995 prices
Objective 1	
Merseyside	663
Objective 2	
North East England	532
West Cumbria	45
Yorkshire and Humberside	544
East Midlands	143
West Midlands	651
Manchester/Lancs/Cheshire	584
East London	139
Thanet	25
Plymouth	52
South Wales	322
Eastern Scotland	205
Western Scotland	473
Industrial Community Initiatives	
RECHAR (coal areas)	165
RESIDER (steel areas)	42
RETEX (textile areas)	36
KONVER (defence areas)	110
Total	**4,731**

Source: Coalfield Communities Campaign/Department of Trade and Industry.

2. Subsidiarity. Clear delegation of decision-making to ensure maximum efficiency and responsibility (but in the UK the doctrine of subsidiarity is not commonly applied below the level of the nation state, whatever is the case in other European countries);
3. Additionality. EC funds should be used in addition to (not instead of) nation state funds. That is to say, the recipients of such funding must 'match' the amount received by an equivalent amount furnished from their own resources. (But government has frequently tried to manipulate or side-step this, as we have already noted.)

The funds made available to the UK for the years (1994-9) under EC Structural Funds have been roughly as shown in Table 9.

These funds have been used in mining areas according to the EURACOM Report *Mining Regions and the Future of EU Regional Aid* for the following purposes:

* developing infrastructure;
* improving the environment;
* setting up and promoting small businesses;
* stimulating indigenous local growth;
* training young people;
* encouraging women in the workplace;
* safeguarding existing jobs and creating employment.

Future Funding

EU regional policy after 1999 is going to be affected by the prospect of the addition of new and even more deprived regions with the expansion of the Union to the East. This will not be a swift process, but it has already led the Commission to propose a concentration of the coverage of EU assisted areas from 51 per cent to 35 per cent/40 per cent of the total Union population, and there will be a slight decline after 1999 in total funding for the EU fifteen. It is expected that areas eligible under Objective 1 will continue to receive assistance, and to receive two-thirds of all funds, but the threshold of 75 per cent of EU average *per capita* GDP will be applied rigorously and in relation to other available funds. Objective 2 funds will be made available for an integrated strategy of economic diversification in regions suffering from structural problems and will be applied to a limited number of identified areas. Coal mining areas are not mentioned in the Commission's statement. Criteria for eligibility are to be 'simpler, transparent and specific", taking account in particular of:
* the rate of unemployment
* the levels of industrial employment
* the level and development of agriculture and the fishing industry
* the degree of social exclusion

Management of funds will be decentralised to Member-states and Regions and a Reserve of 10 per cent will be held back to reward regions with good performance in terms of verifiable results. The Commission report recommends in conclusion:

> 'greater use of other forms of assistance: other grants (interest rate subsidies, guarantees, venture capital holdings, other holdings) in order to better respond to economic needs and take better account of the returns from projects.'

All funds will be combined in a single programme. There will be some transitional support for areas which lose their current eligibility.

Some of the other Objectives are to be merged, but a new Objective 3 is to be introduced for regions not covered by Objectives 1 and 2. This is to develop human resources as a complement to the European Employment Strategy for

* accompanying economic and social changes;
* lifelong education and training systems;
* active labour market policies to fight unemployment;
* combating social exclusion.

Special Initiatives, designed to compensate for the decline of certain industries, will not be renewed as such. Community Initiatives are to be restricted to three, covering

* cross-border co-operation to promote harmonious and balanced spatial planning;
* rural development, and
* human resources with special attention to equal opportunities.

The Cohesion Fund established under the Maastricht Treaty 'to provide a financial contribution to projects in the fields of environment and trans-European networks in the area of transport infrastructure' is to go to member-states whose *per capita* income is less than 90 per cent of the EU average.

Britain's Coalfield Communities Campaign has been working together in EURACOM with representatives from local authorities in mining areas throughout the EU to advance the special claims for continued assistance of the areas they represent. Even though Objective 2 funding has not been abolished altogether, as EURACOM feared, these changes are judged to be bad news for the coalfield areas which have been receiving assistance from European funds. This is true not only for UK coalfields, but for all mining areas in the Union.

RECHAR

The RECHAR Programme has been an important source of European funds for the Coalfields. This was launched in 1990 as a special programme of assistance for the regeneration of the coalfields, drawing from the EC funds. It was devised and lobbied for by the coalfield communities themselves, starting from the first EURACOM conference in 1988. A co-ordinating and sponsoring centre for RECHAR was then designed in DG XVI, the Regional Policy Division of the European Commission, under the leadership of Commissioner Bruce Millan and Programme Director Graham Meadows. The priority in the programme was moved from such measures as the provision of industrial units and community amenities, which had lost their Coal Industry subsidy, to a broader concept of Community Economic Development (CED). This was designed (according to the Lloyd Report):

> 'to concentrate resources on those pockets of exceptional deprivation within eligible regions whose disadvantages are so serious that they face the prospect of long-term social and economic exclusion from the mainstream. The Priority seeks to involve local communities and businesses fully in the process of rejoining the mainstream...'

Community Economic Development works in three ways to encourage local communities to engage in the regeneration process.
* through 'capacity building' of individuals and local organizations to plan and implement strategies;
* through 'programme bending' to use resources in accordance with the desires and needs of the communities;
* through 'community linkage' to reduce isolation from other communities, both those that are similarly deprived and those with greater economic opportunities.

RECHAR 1 ran from 1990-1995 and brought some 300m ECUs of new investment to mining areas.

The main RECHAR 2 Programme runs from 1995-1997 and was due to provide 400m ECUs of aid. Determined lobbying led by the Coalfields Communities Campaign, and intense pressure from within the European Parliament to extend the RECHAR Programme to 1999 has, so far, yielded only a further 45m ecu for the whole of the European coalfields for 1998-99. Parliament resolved in 1996 that this figure should be increased to 100m ecu, but by September 1997 this increment had still not been achieved. Such special Community initiatives, linked to the decline of specific industries, could quite possibly be the first casualties of the reform of the Structural Funds. Table 10 shows, as an example, grants requested and funding available for the UK East Midlands Region from the major part of the RECHAR Programme.

There can be no doubt from the evidence on the ground that community development, with a large educational element at its core,

Table 10
European Funds for UK Coalfields 1995-1997: East Midlands

RECHAR II	Round 1 Allocations (ERDF)			Round 2 Allocations (ERDF)		
	No. of Projects	Grants requested £	Euro funding available £	No. of Projects	Grants requested £	Euro funding available £
M1 Environmental Improvements	43	11,103,703	3,309,000	19	6,191,143	4,781,652
M2 New Work-space	35	7,962,418	2,708,000	20	4,798,258	3,743,686
M3 Tourism	46	10,822,627	1,461,000	21	4,685,174	1,992,964
M4 Access to Economic Opportunities	18	5,310,447	1,504,000	32	9,208,062	2,770,189
M5 SMEs	60	4,930,842	602,000	20	1,516,179	1,008,099
M6 Local Community Infrastructure	44	4,198,705	602,000	22	1,698,514	839,709
Totals	246	44,328,742	10,186,000	134	28,097,330	15,136,299

Source: Government Office for the East Midlands.

is indispensable to the recovery of hope for the future of the coalfields. While the RECHAR money, some of which has gone in the past into industrial units, small scale factory development and the renovation of village halls and community centres, has been of value, the new switch of priority to community development is extremely important. This kind of development is a long process of step by step building. The Lloyd Report distinguished Level One communities where local capacity is relatively undeveloped and Level Two communities where plans have already been formulated and communities are in a position to make a contribution to regeneration. The first are among the most deprived and cannot be expected to move on to Level Two much before current funding runs down. There will be the need by then for much increased funding for education and training to build on what has already been achieved. And even then community development and educational programmes can only be widely effective within a regional, national and European plan for full employment.

Will it be possible for the coalfields to obtain funding under Objective 1?

It has been reported that South Yorkshire hopes to qualify for Objective 1 status, because its GDP is now down to 74 per cent of the average across the European Community. In Britain as a whole, GDP runs at 99 per cent of the average in the European Union. The South Yorkshire bid, at the moment, hovers on the margins, because, taking a three year running average, its percentage of European GDP runs at 76 per cent.

Eurostat, together with other departments of the European Commission, established the units of measurement for regional funds of this kind. They are called NUTS, or Nomenclature of Territorial Units for Statistics. There are five tiers of NUTS:

* NUTS 1 equals Country.
* NUTS 2 equals Region.
* NUTS 3 equals County.
* NUTS 4 equals District.
* NUTS 5 equals Ward.

It is of course, NUTS 2 which applies in the case of South Yorkshire. Local planners are in general agreement about the widespread anomalies which exist in the application of this system. In the South Wales coalfield, or in far off Devon and Cornwall, rich and poor areas are not only adjacent to one another, but surround one another. When we raised this question with the East Midlands Government Office, and asked for a revision of boundaries, to reflect the fact that one particular area shared a whole range of economic circumstances with the adjacent area across a Local Government boundary, we appealed for the compilation of data down to the level of Enumeration District. This is the lowest level at which the census provides figures. We were informed that if this practice were adopted, it would produce a 'pepper-pot effect'. That is to say, we could expect to find concentrations of poverty dotted about the map, in-between other areas of relative comfort or even affluence. A common sense answer to this objection would, of course, insist that if the distribution is a 'pepper-pot' one, then it is in no less need of effective public recognition and action than is a large continuous area sharing the same doleful characteristics.

This question clearly applies to the South Yorkshire application for Objective 1 status. A much wider area of general poverty now stretches southwards from South Yorkshire, across districts of Derbyshire and Northern Nottinghamshire. We have already noted that the disposable income of Ashfield and Mansfield jointly rank 413th out of 438 in the British distribution. There are also very serious concentrations of poverty and acute hardship in the region of Worksop, in parts of North Eastern Derbyshire and as far over as Newark and Sherwood.

But the British data reporting on GDP is presented only down to the level of Counties, so that commuter suburbs cancel out dire want in inner city areas or in destitute coalfield areas. The resultant average cannot be said to be meaningless: it is a deceitful mask which prevents us from looking reality in the face. In fact, an enlarged South Yorkshire/Nottinghamshire/Derbyshire zone houses some of the most distressing misery to be found in the United Kingdom.

Of course, it is very difficult for districts to arrive at data which can prove this point. Meaningful figures of local GDP are difficult to compile because it becomes necessary to distinguish between where people live, work, or spend their money. Already, the regional GDP figures report on the incomes of people living in the region, but the County figures involve only people working in the County.

To resolve these problems would certainly bring full employment to our statisticians. But it is surely worthwhile to make this effort if we can win not only recognition, but serious funding, to the areas of desperation which are involved here.

Even if Objective 1 status might be in reach of South Yorkshire, basing ourselves on the situation in the late nineties, the sand is running out of the hourglass, however. Under Agenda 2000, the enlargement of the European Union entails the early accession of a number of Eastern European countries. The GDP of the four front running candidates is 32 per cent of the European Union average. It becomes entirely clear that the widening of the European Union will either involve a steeply stepped access with diminished entitlements, or substantially new arrangements for funding, whether by taxing or borrowing. Coalfield communities will feel an instinctive sympathy with those beyond the pale, because they are experiencing all the pain of internal exile themselves.

CHAPTER NINE

The Case for Future Funding

The coalfield areas of the United Kingdom have still, by mid-1997, much above national average unemployment, and the gap between the unemployment rate in the pit villages and the national rate is still wider. This is evident even from the official figures of registered claimants. The reality is much worse, because we know that in these areas there is an equal number of hidden unemployed, those men with savings or an illness that keep them off the register, the temporary trainees and those women and older men who no longer trouble to claim. The concentration of unemployment in areas of declining industry, where not only coal mining, but steel making, ship building, agriculture and fishing are all in decline, makes the process of industrial regeneration particularly intractable.

With high long term unemployment there is widespread poverty. Average household incomes in the coalfield areas are much lower than the average in the country and, among the unemployed households, weekly expenditure is less than half the average. For many families with children, incomes are so low as to bring them within the official definition of poverty. Nearly a third of the country's children are in families thus defined and a high proportion of these are in the coalfield areas. By all the other statistical tests of poverty – mortality rates, education after 16, car ownership, ability to afford a holiday, coalfield areas still show up badly. There is simply no evidence of any diminution in the social and economic exclusion which followed upon the decline of the coal and associated industries in the UK, as far as most of the areas that were worst affected. And there is every expectation of more job losses in the coal industry to come.

At the same time, the efforts at self-help in each of the coalfield areas has shown what can be done with an absolute minimum of financial assistance from outside. A few thousand men and women have been assisted to take part in starting a process of regeneration in their communities. It is a story of great courage and imagination. But the scale is very small. Around them in their villages and towns there are hundreds of thousands without jobs or with insecure jobs; and beyond them in the coalfield areas alone a total population of some five millions, many of whom feel that they live deprived lives in an environment that does not get better but seems always to get worse.

Even with the best of efforts from animateurs and local government officers and councillors and in communities that have not yet entirely lost their community sense, people cannot be expected to pull themselves up by their own bootstraps. The situation in the coalfields will not get better without a major public and private investment not only in human skills but in local employment. We made particular reference earlier in this book to the energy conservation work which is underway in the village of Boughton in Nottinghamshire. One of the best ways of creating employment is to improve the insulation of the housing stock and the care and protection of the environment. The initial cost is soon made good by the savings in fuel consumption and the reduction of damage by pollution. To replicate energy villages like Boughton throughout the country would save far more in energy costs than the interest on the initial investment in the work to be done. And that is only one example of many of the ideas that rest in the files of local government offices awaiting only for funding for their realisation.

The European Coal and Steel Community

There is one particular source of funds from which, in justice and in logic, help should come for the regeneration of the coalfields and neighbouring areas of iron and steel production. This is the European Coal and Steel Community (ECSC), which was the foundation stone of European integration and is the most supra-national of all the European institutions, in that it can treat directly with the people it supports, and not indirectly through the Member Governments, as is the case with all other EU institutions. It ends its life after fifty years in the year 2002, and discussion is underway in the ECSC Consultative Committee, the European Parliament and elsewhere concerning the effects of its demise on the workers, the companies and the areas of Europe which were chiefly involved in coal and steel production.

Throughout its life the ECSC expenditure has been financed by a levy on sales, which has been used not only to encourage research and training, but to assist in the rationalisation and restructuring of the two industries. This meant in particular, under Article 56 of the ECSC Treaty (Paris), to support retraining measures in order to

'mitigate the devastating effects on employment of the successive stages in restructuring ... and the conversion and diversification of jobs which are being abolished.'

These words are taken from the Explanatory Statement in the European Parliament on a *Report on the incorporation of the ECSC into the budget of the European Communities*, dated 7th October 1996. The statement in support of a motion for the Parliament emphasised the value of the social activities of the ECSC which its author believes

'represent a unique example of a close, direct link between the Community level and the local, even grassroots level to an often greater degree than is the case with most European Social Fund operations.'

Some part of the funding of regeneration has come from the ECSC, and both the memoranda of the ECSC Consultative Committee (a quadripartite committee of producers, consumers, governments and workers) of 28.06.95 and 10.10.96 and the European Parliament Committee report strongly recommended that the social activities financed in the past by the ECSC should be continued, and adequate funding be provided as ECSC activities are phased out by the year 2002.

In a letter from Commissioner Christos Papoutsis to Ken Coates, MEP, of 16.01.97, the following assurance was given as a 'matter of consensus between the different actors involved':

'As for the social provisions of the ECSC Treaty, with the exception of the phasing-in of the training measures into the ESF (European Structural Fund of European Union, i.e. not the ECSC), it is considered that they should continue to operate in full until the expiry of the Treaty in 2002.'

These provisions are detailed, as we have seen, in Article 56, para 2 of the ECSC Treaty of Paris, which states that

'If fundamental changes, not directly connected with the establishment of the common market conditions for the coal or the steel industry should compel some undertakings permanently to discontinue, curtail or change their activities, the Commission on application by the governments concerned:

(a) may facilitate, in the manner laid down in Article 54, either in the industries within its jurisdiction or, with the assent of the Council, in any other industry, the financing of such programmes as it may approve for the creation of new and economically sound activities capable of reabsorbing redundant workers into productive employment.

[Note: Article 54 of the Treaty allows the Commission 'to facilitate the carrying out of investment programmes by granting loans to undertakings or by guaranteeing other loans which they may contract.]

(b) may provide non-repayable aid towards:

* the payment of tide over allowances to workers;
* the payment of allowances to undertakings to enable them to continue paying such workers as may be temporarily laid off as a result of the undertakings' change of activity;
* the financing of vocational training for workers having to change their employment.

The Commission shall make provision of non-repayable aid conditional on the payment by the state concerned of a special contribution of not less than the amount of that aid, unless an exception is authorised by the Council, acting by a two-thirds majority.'

What has all this amounted to in the years 1991-5 which saw the maximum closing down of coal production in the EC, and especially in the UK? It appears from Table 11 below that some 360 million ecus was paid out to 155,300 workers, about half of them in the UK. That is on

Table 11

Traditional Redeployment Aid provided to the UK Coal Industry by ECSC

This assistance is for tideover, resettlement and retraining allowances. It includes contributions to early retirement and severance pay made to British Coal under Treaty Article 56.2 (b).

Year	No. of workers receiving aid		Value in ECUs	
	EC	UK	EC	UK
1991	27,986	7,548	69,942,814	15,385,225
1992	32,042	11,661	80,672,107	23,307,816
1993	32,082	21,002	70,289,753	42,621,000
1994	38,844	22,047	77,147,169	40,999,839
1995	24,401	10,275	64,251,705	22,702,000
Five Year Totals	155,355	72,533	362,303,548	145,015,880

(Extracted from ECSC Annual Financial Reports)

average about 2300 ecus per worker. The maximum sum permitted per worker is 3000 ecus and all ECSC payments are 'conditional on payment by the Member State concerned of at least an equivalent contribution'.

These are all payments made under Article 56.2 (b). Under the wider provision of Article 56.2 (a) contributions were made to the RECHAR programme of about 125 million ecus in both 1994 and 1995, between a third and a quarter of which came to the UK. These are very small sums compared with the annual income of the ECSC from interest and financial operations (over 1000 million ecus) and value of loans disbursed of some 20 billion ecus over a twenty year period. It hardly adds up to what was promised under the ECSC Treaty of Paris.

The Future of ECSC Funding

Moreover, it appears that even the future of these payments is in question. M. Papoutsis in the letter quoted earlier suggested that the Member States were 'legally the heirs to the ECSC reserves' and that restructuring the coal and steel industries of Poland and the Czech Republic would in future be calling for what he called 'social crisis management' and the necessity 'from the outset to provide for the inclusion of these future Member States as beneficiaries'. This argument was at once challenged by Ken Coates on the grounds that the ECSC had been a separate body within the European Communities. Its funds had been built up from the levy payments of the industries which had composed it, with provision specifically made in the Treaty for the event of fundamental changes in market conditions.

The Consultative Committee's memorandum of 28.06.95 recalled that the social dimension of the ECSC Treaty was clearly laid down and reiterated its position that the reserves of the ECSC should be used primarily for the benefit of the undertakings and their workers, since it is they who, since 1952, provided the bulk of the funds enabling the reserves to be constituted.

The ECSC has reserves valued at nearly 700 million ecus, which have been built up from payments made out of the wages and profits of those involved in the two industries over the years. These reserves have been used as collateral for a large programme of borrowing and lending on the open market. ECSC loans outstanding, including sums lent to the Channel Tunnel consortium, amounted in 1996 to some 6 billion ecus. This has been a revolving fund and represents precisely the kind of supra-national financing that was proposed in the Delors Report of 1993 for creating new jobs as a counterweight to the adverse effects on employment of the Maastricht Treaty convergence criteria.

Now, at the turn of the century, this valuable source of supra-national funds for regeneration and cohesion is being phased out just when it is most needed with unemployment levels in many parts of Europe at record levels. The ECSC Consultative Committee was so seized by this fact that it recommended the allocation of the ECSC reserves to 'a financial mechanism (e.g. a foundation)' under the Commission, to manage the use of these funds, and to continue the 'dialogue between producers, workers, consumers on the one hand and the Commission on the other'.

In its memorandum of 10.10.96, the Consultative Committee listed the measures of 'non-repayable aid' that should be provided under article 56.2 (b) of the Treaty, but also noted that, while it recommended in its earlier memorandum of 18.06.95 that adequate resources be provided for by the ECSC operating budget to finance the desired social measures, yet this was to be part of a Community employment strategy, as proposed in the Commission's 1993 White Paper on *Growth, Competitiveness and Employment* (the Delors Report),

> 'it is disappointed that in two specific cases – retraining and aid for subsidised housing – the ECSC measures have been discontinued without any provision being made for continuing them under the general budget' and that 'nothing has been done' to strengthen social cohesion through ECSC-type 'social flanking measures for the Community's sectoral policies'.

There is some disagreement in the European Parliament on the best way to ensure that the social activities of the ECSC are continued after the year 2002. The opinion presented to the Parliament from the Committee on Social Affairs and Employment, while stating that there should be no excuse for cutting expenditure, expected that the ECSC's social responsibilities would be integrated into other EU instruments and insisted only that measures affecting existing workers – early retirement schemes, tideover allowances, wage make-up payments and resettlement allowances – must be met. The Committee on Regional Policy, by contrast, was concerned about the continuing need for readaptation measures as the coal and steel industries continued to shed labour, and about the transfer of responsibilities for vocational training schemes from the ECSC to the Social Fund with no additional financial allocation and no prioritisation for coal and steel workers. This Committee concluded by reiterating Parliament's call in March of 1996 for increased RECHAR and RESIDER funding and by stating its belief that the ECSC reserves should

> 'continue to be used for the benefit of companies and workers where it is still necessary to provide financial support for industrial and employment conversion measures and considers that the Commission should, as a matter of urgency, make concrete proposals to ensure the continuation of the ECSC activities after the expiry of the ECSC Treaty and the creation of an agency to administer the reserves.'

In the event, Member State governments were authorised by the Commission to provide very large sums as aid in support of the coal mining industry in 1995-6. Overall these subsidies amounted to the equivalent of some £7,000 million. But these payments were mainly designed to cover current operating losses of the mining and steel companies, rather than aid to displaced workers or to areas of decline:
* 4,400 million francs (£400 millions) for the French industry as 'compensation for operating losses';
* 13,000 million deutschmarks (£5,000 millions) for the German industry, to 'cover the supply of coal and coke to the Community iron and steel industry' and for 'electricity generation purposes';
* 345 million escudos (£110 millions) to the Portuguese industry for social measures on pit closures;
* 293,000 million pesetas (£1,300 millions) to the Spanish industry for 'sector restructuring', 'operating losses' and 120 million pesetas (sic) for 'social payments'.

Only the very small sum of £40 million was authorised by the Commission for RECHAR and the idea of a 'foundation' for social expenditure from the ECSC's reserves appeared to be dead.

Whatever the ECSC Consultative Committee or the European Parliament may recommend, one can be sure that the outcome will depend on the Ministers, meeting as Finance Ministers, and they will only act in support of the regeneration of areas of widespread industrial decline, if they can find ways of overcoming the restriction on their national budgets which are following from the convergence criteria of the Maastricht Treaty. As with all other aspects of the challenge of mass unemployment in the European Union, a solution must lie with the activation of European-wide borrowing instruments and the political will to support a great extension of their use. There is a particularly powerful case in relation to areas where the coal and related industries were concentrated for establishing an open enquiry into the current and future status of the funding of the European Coal and Steel Community.

A Levy on Imports

Beyond this, there is one obvious source of funding for the areas throughout Europe which have suffered from the arbitrary and precipitate closure of the coal industry, carried out with the aim of taking advantage of the availability of imports of cheap coal and gas, and without any planning of alternative employment. Since the imported coal is being produced either with heavy subsidies, as is said to be the case in the USA and Australia: or with labour paid at below International Labour Organization minimum rates, as in the case of South Africa and Poland, a levy should be imposed upon all imports. This is what is done for agricultural products under the Common Agricultural Policy and could be applied to a Common Fuel Policy. If fuel prices rise, this will encourage better fuel conservation measures and, in the meantime, pensioners and the unemployed can be protected by a special discount on their fuel bills. Europe of the fifteen is currently importing about 140 million tonnes of coal a year, roughly equal to total European production, which only seven years ago was 50 per cent greater. At a £30 a tonne import price a levy of 20 per cent would yield £840 million a year. Such a levy on UK imports of 24 million tonnes would produce £143 million a year, more than doubling current RECHAR funding.

CHAPTER TEN

What is Needed Now

A few hundred million pounds from aid, or levies, is by no means a large sum compared with the annual loss of income to the Coalfield areas which we estimated earlier to amount to some £4,000 million a year. Nor does it begin to compare with the subsidies and compensation paid to the coal industries of Europe while they were still producing at much higher levels. If all State expenditures are to continue to be subject to cutting back so as to meet the Maastricht convergence criteria for Member State budgets to qualify for entry into the Economic and Monetary Union, then it will be urgently necessary for Union-wide steps to be taken to reverse the consequent further spread of mass unemployment throughout Europe. It will be necessary that new Union-wide instruments should be launched, as proposed in the Delors Report, to provide for investment in the 'creation of new and economically sound activities ... capable of reabsorbing the redundant workers into productive employment'. That was the promise of the Paris Treaty in 1952. Today, when the need to fulfil that promise is so urgent, there can be no excuse for reneging.

There is still some uncertainty about the future of ECSC funds, but we understand from Commissioner Papoutsis (see Annexe below), that in future funds are not to be made available for regenerating regions where the coal and steel industries have been largely phased out. If this is so, then more of the responsibility for regeneration falls back upon the Member-states. In this book, we have argued that the UK coalfield areas have suffered particularly heavily from the pit closure programme of the 1990s and that, while redundancy payments have been made and imaginative educational and training programmes have been initiated and progressed, this has not begun to create new jobs on the scale required to offset continuing high levels of unemployment. It is becoming widely recognised – in reports of the ILO, UNCTAD, OECD, and the European Commission – that supply side measures, to make workers more 'employable', are of little use if there is no investment on the demand side in new employment creation. This we saw was the potential weakness of all the community self-help schemes which have grown up in the coalfield.

Public resources have been scant, and stringently rationed, so that local initiatives have been starved of funding in spite of heroic efforts by councillors and volunteers. Private funds have tended to go elsewhere.

Mr Prescott's Promise

No Swedish-style rescue actions were taken by the Conservative Government in Britain to prepare for the shut-down of the greater part of the coal industry over two to three years – a tragedy for which the new Labour deputy prime minister has been upbraiding them in his recent speeches. At the Durham Miners' Gala on July 12th, 1997, Mr Prescott pledged £1 billion 'to build a better future for mining communities which suffered bitterly under the previous Conservative administration ... first by the pit closures, then by unemployment and decline and then a third time, because thanks to underestimated unemployment figures, these communities could lose out on European money.'

The sources of funding which Mr Prescott indicated were:
* increasing help from Europe
* the welfare to work programme
* the environmental task force
* 'our own regeneration funds'
* local authority budgets
* releasing housing capital receipts
* Regional Development Agencies and a new Development Agency currently being legislated for
* the windfall tax from the profits of the utilities.

It is not clear whether any of these, apart from the housing receipts and the windfall tax, would be able to provide any new money. Local Authority and regional agencies were left seriously short of funds by the Conservative Government's last expenditure plans, which Labour has promised not to alter during its first two years of office. After Mr

Prescott's speech, Mr Alan Meale, Mr Prescott's Parliamentary Private Secretary, questioned whether Mr Prescott had mentioned a fund of £1 billion for coalfield regeneration. But one of the journalists who was present has got a tape recording of the speech in which the promise was made. Subsequently, *The Observer* reported (3rd August 1997) that Mr Prescott 'has up to £700 million to spend, mostly from the European Union'. This sounds suspiciously like part of the allocation of 2,500 million ecus to Objective 2 areas, made over a year ago. If that is the case, it is not new money.

The £1 billion, if it were made available, would presumably be spread over a number of years. There is an ominous similarity to the £1 billion promised by Mr Heseltine to coalfield areas when the pit closure programme was announced in 1992. This was never clearly accounted for, but, apart from redundancy payments to miners out of ECSC redundancy funds, it seems not to have amounted, as we saw earlier, to much more than £400 million, mostly under the RECHAR programme, which is coming to an end.

The omens for 'increasing help from Europe' do not look too promising. The draft budget of the European Union for 1998 was approved by the Council of Ministers on July 25th 1997, after they had cut one billion ecus from the Structural Fund appropriations which had been recommended by the Commission. The overall budget amounts to 1.13 per cent of the EU's GNP, well below the agreed ceiling of 1.26 per cent. Instead of a 3 per cent increase in line with inflation proposed by the Commission, the Ministers decided to continue their 'zero growth' imposed in 1997. Only the provisions for Objective 1 regions, the most disadvantaged ones mainly in Southern Europe, Objective 6 regions (Finland and Sweden) and the Cohesion Fund for Spain, Portugal and Greece were exempted after strong protests came from these regions. As a result, funds destined for those purposes were ring-fenced, so that disproportionately larger cuts had to be made in others: education, vocational training and youth programmes, in information and communications and other social actions and in energy.

Agence Europe reported that general satisfaction was shared by the 'net contributing states', which include the UK. 'For Mrs. Helen Liddell, Economic Secretary to the British Treasury', the report added, the draft budget was 'an encouraging start to this year's EC budget round and good news for the taxpayer'.

'Budget discipline', she went on, 'is gaining ground in Europe. I and my colleagues today marked our determination to keep European spending under the same rigorous constraints as our national budgets ...'

Good news for the higher income taxpayer: bad news for the unemployed!

More Cuts or Regeneration

The Ministers' decision does not necessarily end the matter, because the delegation from the European Parliament opposed the cuts and the Parliament has reserve powers over the EU budget, which can still be used. The Ministers took their decision by a qualified majority, with the Mediterranean Member-states voting against; and Members of the European Parliament can argue that the cuts go against the unanimous decision of the Edinburgh European Council in 1992 to maintain the level of appropriations under the Structural Funds.

Cuts in the European Structural Funds also mean cuts in national funding, because Member-states are required to contribute 50:50 counterpart payments when receiving appropriations. Since the main cuts are to fall on Objective 2 regions, Britain's coalfields will be the worst hit as major beneficiaries from this funding. It would seem that some of the £1 billion that John Prescott promised for the coalfields at the Durham Miners' Gala could be taken away by his colleague, Mrs Liddell, unless the Euro MPs can successfully support the Commission against the Ministers.

We have seen that there can be no doubt that the needs of the British coalfields which Mr Prescott was addressing are dire, and that the help he is offering would be essential if we were to prevent the exclusion of whole communities. Mr Prescott promised to convene a special conference of English Partnerships and representatives of the coalfield communities. They will want to see a plan for regeneration that really makes good the devastation of the last five years and more. This will not be achieved without Government money in grants and loans to invest in replacing the jobs that have been lost. Private capital will not flow in unless there is a guaranteed major input into the infrastructure and into the renewal of run-down housing, schools and hospitals and general amenities. To these public investments should be added direct public expenditure on job creation. This is where modernisation should be working.

Public enterprise need not necessarily be confined to bureaucratic National Boards. It can be generated up from the roots, by joining the forces of Local Authorities. A coalfield development consortium, linking the main Local Authorities, could, given significant funding, promote both public enterprise in a variety of fields, and the encouragement of private initiatives.

There are proposals emerging from Mr Prescott's office for Regional Development Agencies, but without new funding they appear to be mainly providing a tidying-up operation co-ordinating the several existing quangos. They also lack democratic accountability except in the cases of Scotland and Wales. The destruction of the old coalfield economy cannot be allowed to destroy the future of our communities, and local democracy can best help the work of recovery by pioneering new projects in local socialism, new joint co-operatives, and new joint production corporations to fill the voids that private capitalism cannot see, or will not reach.

Afterwood

s in Sedgefield in 1983, so today a large proportion of the unemployed in the coalfields are under twenty-five years of age. And as Tony Blair told us in 1983:

> 'Those young people are not merely faced with a temporary inability to find work. For many, the dole queue is their first experience of adult life. For some, it will be their most significant experience. Without work, they do not merely suffer the indignity of enforced idleness – they wonder how they can afford to get married, to start a family, and to have access to all the benefits of society that they should be able to take for granted. Leisure is not something that they enjoy, but something that imprisons them.'

Of course it is right to offer all these people access to further education, and to training in appropriate skills. We have examined some aspects of this problem, with a view to learning from present practice and the limitations from which it has suffered. But we have also seen that training which is divorced from the possibility of real employment is ultimately a tormenting frustration. And the promotion of suitable employment is a matter of the planned deployment of resources, both public and private. The idea that the market will rectify all the sufferings of the coalfields may just possibly be true if one takes an unacceptably long view. But, as Lord Keynes told us,

> 'In the long run, we are all dead.'

The coalfields were not imprisoned in single-industry dependency by the market. They were planned into monopoly employment conditions, by strict and active governmental intervention. All parties connived in this process, and none can escape the consequent responsibilities. Government intervention imprisoned miners' sons in the coal industry when the entire national future depended on coal. Today, even the vestigial industry which survived the 1992-3 closure programme is in jeopardy. As we write, Asfordby mine in the Vale of Belvoir, is undergoing all the traumas of closure. There is an anguished debate about which we will have more to say elsewhere. But the proposed closure of Asfordby is clearly linked with the future of the rest of the industry. New guarantees are being sought to assure a future market for coal. It is in the highest degree unlikely that these guarantees will be provided by a non-interventionist Government which is largely driven by conformity to market forces. The Norwegians have just discovered a major new gas field, which promises a possibility of formidable reductions in the price of natural gas, which in turn might well bring about the end of all coal mining in Britain.

We do not know whether coal will, or will not, survive this new competition. But we have shown that there is still much to be done in the coalfields now, before all can, in Tony Blair's words, participate in the benefits of the common weal. If our people are to survive, it is necessary to plan for economic recovery in the coalfields, and to bring to bear powerful new resources. The present political power has reached high office on the hopes of millions of forgotten people, hundreds of thousands of whom live in the coalfields. When can they expect to see an effort to repay the debts which have been incurred?

Correspondence

3rd December 1996

Commissioner Christos Papoutis
European Commission
Rue de la Loi 200
Brussels
Belgium

Dear Christos,
Ludivina Garcia Arias has asked me to help her prepare a report for EURACOM on the need for new programmes of assistance to declining coalfield areas.

I am collecting the necessary papers, but I badly need a briefing on the state of affairs concerning the resources of the European Coal and Steel Community and current proposals for their use.

Can you help me? Is there anything you can send me?

With every good wish.

Yours sincerely,
Ken Coates

16th January 1997

Dear Ken,
Thank you for your letter of 3rd December in which you ask for a briefing on the state of affairs concerning the resources of the European Coal and Steel Community and the current proposals for their use. Let

me summarize the key elements.

Further to the Communication from the Commission to the Council of 15th March 1991 on 'The Future of the ECSC Treaty' (SEC(91) 407 final) a number of general principles have been established, which are a matter of consensus between the different actors involved and which have been repeatedly accepted by the Consultative Committee and the European Parliament:

*   The ECSC Treaty should remain in force until the year 2002 as an autonomous legal instrument.
*   The principles governing State Aid for the ECSC sectors should continue to be applied until the year 2002. With respect to coal mining, the current rules on aid, set out in Decision 3632/93/ECSC are considered to be an adequate instrument for energy policy, taking into account its social and regional impact.
*   As for the social provisions of the ECSC Treaty, with the exception of the phasing-in of the training measures into the ESF, it is considered that they should continue to operate in full until the expiry of the Treaty in 2002.

In the field of research, where the Commission has envisaged a phasing-in into the Framework Programme, it has recently been suggested (by the Consultative Committee, among others) that a special mechanism be set up to finance sectoral research after the expiry of the ECSC Treaty, with a view to ensuring the continuation of both coal and steel research as a precondition for maintaining competitiveness, export markets and hence thousands of jobs in fields like mining technology.

This matter is directly linked to the question of resources and financial activities, and more specifically to the way in which outstanding ECSC loans should be guaranteed after 2002. Further to a report by the 'ECSC 2002' working party, the Commission's position can currently be described as follows:

*   It is advisable to maintain the AAA rating of ECSC bonds after the Treaty expires and to keep, with a view to maintaining this rating, a level of reserves covering 100 per cent of the loans outstanding after 2002 that do not have a government guarantee.
*   Using the reserves needed to guarantee the loans not covered by a government guarantee (ECU 670 million), it is suggested that a fund generating interest which might be used to finance research in the coal and steel sectors be set up.

*   As the interest from this fund will be necessarily a diminishing amount, it could also be envisaged that some of the reserves released when the ECSC loans expire, be reallocated to this fund.

The next step is now for the Commission to draft – on the basis of that position – a Communication to the Council that should be on the agenda of one of the Industry Councils in the first half of 1997.

I consider that the opportunity should be taken to give the discussion on the future of the ECSC a broader perspective. In the event that the Member States – who are legally the heirs to the ECSC reserves – would consider creating an instrument to finance coal and steel research after 2002, it would start its work at exactly the same time as a number of new Member States (i.e. the countries of Central Europe) are expected to join the Union. In order to avoid any discrimination against these countries, it would therefore be necessary from the outset to provide for the inclusion of these future Member States as beneficiaries.

On the other hand, I personally believe that there is an urgent need for the discussions on the future of the ECSC to take into account the tremendous changes in the solid fuels and steel sectors that the next enlargement will bring about. By the year 2002, the coal production of Poland and the Czech Republic will far outweigh total EU-15 production, and will at the same time be confronted with the same structural problems our industry has experienced over the last three decades.

In the steel sector, the competition from the CEECs with important overcapacities will become a major challenge for EU-15 industry, leading to fundamental changes in market conditions.

I believe that, provided this idea wins ground, it would be wise to enable any proposed mechanism – on top of support for sectoral research – to tackle at least part of the problem for the coal and steel industry, created by the enlargement, in the light of the experience gained within the ECSC over the last decades including: social crisis management in connection with restructuring programmes, technical assistance in the field of reconversion and redeployment measures etc. This would have a higher political relevance and might convince some Member States to endorse the creation of such an instrument.

I hope the information and the suggestions made will be of some assistance for you.

If you have further questions for factual information on the ongoing discussions concerning the ECSC, please feel free to contact me.

Yours sincerely,
Christos Papoutsis

24th January 1997

Mr Christos Papoutsis, Commissioner for Energy
The European Commission

Dear Christos,

Thank you so much for your letter of the 16th January, briefing me on the present state of affairs concerning the resources of the European Coal and Steel Community, and current proposals for their deployment.

Your letter was certainly very clear, and enables me to focus down on the issues which still perplex me.

The third of the general consensual principles which you enunciate, concerning the period between now and the year 2002, holds that the social provisions of the ECSC Treaty 'should continue to operate in full' until expiry. (Of course, I have noted what you say about the exception concerning the phase-in of training measures to the European Social Fund.)

This commitment to continue to operate the social provisions raises matters of immense importance to the declining coalfields, and those which have recently closed. Ludivina Garcia Arias has asked me to prepare a report on the outstanding problems of these areas, and I have made considerable progress in documenting the situation which currently obtains in the British coalfields. I have no doubt that in other Member-states there are areas afflicted by the same conditions. And I fear that coalfields which have survived up to now will come under the same threat in the near future.

In a nutshell, I should say that my investigations establish, beyond any reasonable doubt, that the British coalfields which have suffered extensive mine closures are enduring widespread poverty, some of which is acute and socially devastating. There are very high levels of long-term unemployment, and youth unemployment has become a dire problem. In due course, if you have the time to look at it, I will send you my report on these matters, but I suspect that you are already familiar with the burden of these and associated complaints.

It is in this connection that I have been concerned with the continued validity of Article 56 of the ECSC Treaty. This says that the Commission 'may facilitate, in the manner laid down in Article 54, either in the industries within its jurisdiction or, with the assent of the Council, in any other industry, the financing of such programmes as it may approve for the creation of new and economically sound activities capable of reabsorbing the redundant workers into productive employment'.

In the past the Commission made generous contributions in respect of the other provisions laid down in this same article concerning redundancy, resettlement and vocational training. But the essential question today is: what can be done about the physical replacement of an industry which has actually collapsed? This issue was very much in the minds of those who drafted the Treaty of Paris, because in the same Article 56, they revert to the issue in section 2(a) which insists again, in the very same words, on the same points.

Article 54, twice cited in these provisions, allows the Commission to facilitate investment programmes, to grant loans to undertakings, or to guarantee other loans which they may have contracted. If I read the article correctly, every item of activity sanctioned in Article 56 would be covered by the provisions of Article 54.

Is my reading of these two articles correct?

Has this question been considered in the deliberations of the Commission and the Consultative Committee? If so, what conclusion did they reach? If not, was there any impediment which was felt to prevent such consideration?

If, in the light of the social provisions of the European Coal and Steel Community, action were sought on these provisions of Articles 56 and 54, how do you think this would affect the points on page 2 in your letter concerning the maintenance of reserves to cover ECSC bonds? And indeed, would there be any impediment to raising further loans to be applied for the purpose of economic regeneration in the destroyed coalfields?

Would it be possible to consider this issue in preparing the Commission's draft of the Communication to the Council which you mention as being due in the first half of 1997? I wonder if you could also explain to me how the Member-states have become the legal heirs of the ECSC reserves? I would have thought that the industries whose levy payments accumulated these funds might reasonably assert a prior claim over the Member-states who were not so directly involved in building up the funds disposed of by that community. You will note that the Consultative Committee, in its Memorandum 95/C206/06, reiterates its position that the reserves of the ECSC should be used primarily for the benefit of the undertakings and their workers, since it is they who, since 1952, have provided the bulk of the funds enabling the reserves to be constituted.

Of course, this also raises the question which you have explained so clearly, about the possible use of ECSC funds to ease the transition of coal and steel producers in Eastern Europe to membership of the Union. I need to think about this, and will write to you later on the matter. But I would really be most grateful if you could give me your views about the possibility of action on the social provisions of the ECSC Treaty along the lines suggested in this letter.

With very many thanks for all your help.

Yours sincerely,

Ken Coates

24th April 1997

Ken Coates, MEP,
European Parliament

Dear Ken,

Thank you for your letter of the 24th January 1997 in which you raise a number of additional questions concerning the future of the ECSC Treaty. Firstly, I would like to stress that the idea of an extension of the Treaty was ruled out by all the European Union institutions, and therefore it will expire in July 2002. It is clear that this puts some constraints on the use of the ECSC financial instruments to finance reconversion measures for coal and steel regions. In fact, it was decided to stop granting new ECSC conversion loans as of the middle of this year, because it would not be reasonable to have such loans extending over a period of less than five years.

The main challenge for the coal and steel regions is the problem of economic redevelopment. The Commission within the framework of the Structural Funds and the Community initiatives is committed to a policy in favour of regions affected by declining industries. The special measures in the framework of the RECHAR II programme have been extended to 1999. In parallel, the services of DG XVII are currently discussing with DG V the extension of the complementary social programme for coal under Article 56 of the ECSC Treaty.

However, the possibilities for the effective use of ECSC readaptation aid are diminishing, taking into account the age structure of the residual workforce in coal companies in the European Union. For workers under 40 years of age the emphasis today is on training and job creation. To conclude, there is little chance that the remaining reserves of the ECSC could be used entirely for social and regional measures within the European Union before the expiry of the Treaty.

As regards your question on the ECSC reserves, it has been repeatedly confirmed by our Legal Service that the member-states are the legal heirs of the reserves after the expiry of the Treaty, which is a consequence of international law.

I would like to take the occasion to underline the fact that the economic and social situation of the future Member-states of Central Europe is quite similar to the conditions prevailing in Western Europe in the 1950s and 1960s. The scale of possible job losses in these countries is certainly comparable to what has been experienced in the regions of the European Union that suffered most from the decline of the coal industry.

That is why, without prejudging the nature of future action in this field, it is clear that these problems will have to be taken into account in the pre-enlargement perspective. However, it goes without saying that initiatives in favour of the economic regeneration of European Union coalfields will remain a political priority, and that whatever structure might be set up for administering the reserves after the expiry of the ECSC Treaty, should among other things, contribute to easing the social and regional problems of the coalfields both in the European Union and in the future Member-states.

Yours sincerely,
Christos Papoutsis

After Amsterdam

At the Summit in Amsterdam, the proposal (of dubious legality?) to 'return' the assets of the European Coal and Steel Community to the Member-states was not accepted. Instead, the European Council resolved that the Commission should establish a Research Fund 'for sectors related to the coal and steel industries'.

Subsequently, the Commission set out its proposals in a communication (IP/97/861) dated 8 October 1997. It said:

'It is proposed that the Member States, the direct heirs to the ECSC, should decide unanimously to transfer these assets to the Communities remaining. In order to ensure that all the revenue generated by these assets, which will come to around ECU 40 million a year, is used for coal and steel research, the sums would be placed in an autonomous internal fund to be administered by the Commission in association with the sectors concerned.

Coal
Support should be extended to growth sectors associated with coal where technological progress can create jobs. The scope of research should be enlarged from hard coal to other associated solid fuels, primarily brown coal and biomass. Two large sectors involving many small and medium sized businesses would also be concerned: coal combustion and conversion technologies and mining technologies in the broad sense.

Steel
In addition to the production and use of steel, activities in which small businesses are heavily involved (first stage processing, not currently covered by ECSC research), scrap recuperation and preparation and targeted innovation schemes and measures to exploit research results would also be concerned. Pilot and demonstration projects would continue. Hygiene, health and safety at the workplace and environmental matters would be maintained in post 2002 research under the conditions currently prevailing both for coal research and steel research.'

References

Beatty, Christina & Fothergill, Stephen, *Registered and Hidden Unemployment in the UK Coalfields*, Sheffield Hallam University, 1996.

Beatty, Christina, Fothergill, Stephen & Lawless, Paul, *Geographical Variation in the Labour Market Adjustment Process: The UK Coalfields, 1981-91*, Sheffield Hallam University, 1995.

Beatty, Christina, Fothergill, Stephen, Gore, Tony & Herrington, Alison, *The Real Level of Employment*, Sheffield Hallam University, 1997.

Blair, Tony, 'Maiden Speech' on the Finance Bill, House of Commons, *Official Report*, 6 July, 1983.

British Coal Corporation, *Annual Report, 1994*.

British Medical Association, *British Medical Journal*, Editorial, August 1992.

Central Statistical Office, *Census of Population, 1991*, HMSO, 1994.
Regional Trends, 1995-1997.
Family Expenditure Surveys.

Coalfield Communities Campaign, *A Manifesto for the Coalfields*, Barnsley, 1991.
A Fair Deal for Coal – A Fair Deal for Britain, Barnsley, 1997.
The UK Coalfields: A Social Audit, Barnsley, 1997.

Coates, Ken & Silburn, Richard, *Poverty, The Forgotten Englishman*, Harmondsworth, 1970.

Coates, Ken (Ed.), *The Right to Work*, Spokesman, Nottingham, 1995.

Cooke, Heather, *Shirebrook: A Sociological Review*, Bolsover Diamond Regeneration Programme, 1995.

Derbyshire County Council, *Development Plan*, 1960.
Monthly Unemployment Statistics.
Colliery Closures: Impact Study, October 1992.
North Derbyshire Coalfield: Rural Development Area Operating Plan, 1995/6 to 1997/8 Submission to the Rural Development Commission, October 1994.
Derbyshire's Last Three Pits: A Survey of Redundant Mineworkers, April 1995 and An Update, October 1996.
Poverty in Derbyshire, No.4: Unemployment, Welfare Rights Service, 1994.
Derbyshire Job Centre Vacancy. Survey, 1996, January 1997.
DCC Mobile Project Development Plan 1996-7 and *North East Derbyshire Mobile Project Annual Report, 1995*.

English Partnerships, *Partnership Opportunities in England's Coalfields*, Newton-le-Willows, 1997.

EUR-ACOM, *The Social Problems of Coalfield Communities*, Barnsley, September 1991.
Mining Regions and the Future of EU Regional Aid, Barnsley, 1996.

European Coal and Steel Community, *Treaty of Paris*, 1952
Financial Report 1995, Luxemburg, 1996.

European Commission, *Communication from the Commission to the Council and to the European Parliament: Future of the ECSC Treaty*, March 1991.
Commission Decision Establishing Community Rules for State Aid to the Coal Industry, Brussels, 28 December 1993.
Regional Development Studies; New Location Factors for Mobile Investment in Europe, Brussels, 1994.
Competitiveness and Cohesion Trends in the Regions, Brussels, 1994.
7th Annual Report on the Structural Funds, 1995, Brussels, 1996.
Social and Economic Inclusion through Regional Development, Report of Committee, chaired by Prof. Peter Lloyd, Brussels, 1996.
Non-Nuclear Energy (Joule-Thermie), 1994-1998, Brussels, 1996.

European Parliament, *Report and Resolution: on the Incorporation of the ECSC into the Budget of the European Communities*, Brussels, October 1996.

Fothergill, Stephen & McAvan, Linda, *The Social Problems of Coal Areas*, Sheffield Hallam University, 1993.

Goad, R. and Fotherby, J.R., Joint Presentation to John Prescott, Mansfield & Bolsover District Councils, 6 October 1997.

Guy, N., *Dole not Coal: Redundant Miners Survey*, Coalfield Communities Campaign, Barnsley, 1994.

Halstead, John & Wright, Philip, *Confronting Industrial Demise*, University of Sheffield Division of Adult Continuing Education, 1995.

Knapton, Chris, *Sherwood Energy Village – Outline: The World's First Autonomous nett zero CO_2 Emissions Industrial Community*, Energy Advocates, 1995.

North Derbyshire TEC, *Annual Report 1995-6*, Chesterfield, 1996.

North Nottinghamshire TEC, *Final Coal Plan Evaluation, Final Report*, September 1997.

Northern Institute for Continuing Education, *Coalfields Learning Project Operational Plan, 1996-1998*, Northern College, Barnsley, 1996.
Coalfields Learning Project Annual Report 1995-6, Northern College, 1996

Nottinghamshire County Council, *West Nottinghamshire Town Map, 1963-81*, Nottingham, 1963.
Nottinghamshire Rural Development Area: Annual Review 1995, Nottingham, 1995
Nottinghamshire Rural Development Area Strategy: A Submission to the Rural Development Commission, 1994, Nottingham, 1994.
Fast Forward in Nottinghamshire, Nottingham, 1996.
Employment Bulletin, 1995-1997.

Nottingham University, *The Three Mines Study*, Trent Regional Health Authority, 1994.

Rowntree Trust, *Redundant Coal Miners in the Doncaster Area of Yorkshire*, Economic and Social Research Council, 1993.

Shirebrook & District Development Trust, *Patchwork News*, monthly 1995-97.
Portfolio, 1995.
Skills Audit, 1996.

Smith, Jillian, 'The OPCS Longitudinal Study', *Social Trends 26*, HMSO, 1996.

Webster, David, *Travel to Work Areas and Local Unemployment Statistics: A Glasgow View*, Glasgow City Housing, 1997.

West Nottinghamshire Technical College, *Course Guide 1996/7*, Mansfield, 1996.

Witt, S., *When the Pit Closes*, Coalfield Communities Campaign, Barnsley, 1990.